MAIN

STREET

NORTHEASTERN OREGON

The Founding and Development of Small Towns

by
Barbara Ruth Bailey

OREGON HISTORICAL SOCIETY

Production of this volume was supported by funds provided by the Autzen Foundation, the Julian Cheatham Foundation, Crown Zellerbach Corporation, Evans Products Corporation, the S. S. Johnson Foundation, the Malarkey Foundation, the Templeton Foundation, the Wheeler Foundation and the Weyerhaeuser Foundation.

Library of Congress Cataloging in Publication Data

Bailey, Barbara Ruth, 1944-
  Main Street, northeastern Oregon

  Bibliography: p.
  Includes index
  1. Cities and towns—Oregon—Growth—History. 2. Streets—Oregon—
  History. I. Title.
HT123.5.07B34   307.7'62'097957   80-84483
ISBN 0-87595-105-8   AACR2
ISBN 0-87595-073-6 (pbk.)

Printed in the United States of America

Contents

Illustrations

Tables

Foreword

THIS IS A STUDY of a region and the towns within it. Because of its distance and contrast from the Willamette Valley, Oregon's economic hub, northeastern Oregon is seldom emphasized in discussions of the state. But the region, a beautiful part of Oregon, deserves recognition in its own right. The small towns within northeastern Oregon, with their intriguing main streets, also merit attention. This study, therefore, has been devoted to the growth and development of these small towns' main streets; in order to identify their setting, regional and town development is also discussed.

This volume examines all of the towns founded within the region, surviving and failed, except two. The exceptions, Baker and La Grande, each with a population of around 10,000, are about four times larger than the next largest town, Enterprise. This size difference excluded them from this work. But Baker and La Grande underwent many experiences similar to those of the smaller towns of the region. Perhaps someday someone will take the ideas formulated here and extend them to the development of these two cities.

As a geographical region, northeastern Oregon is well defined by both natural boundaries and county lines. It is enclosed by the Blue Mountains to the west and north, the Snake River to the east, and the Burnt River to the south. The region is bordered by the states of Washington to the north and Idaho to the east. It consists of Union, Wallowa and Baker counties. Umatilla County, west of the Blues, is sometimes considered part of northeastern Oregon. However, in terms of its history, development and economy, it is more closely related to the dry wheat country of the Columbia Basin than to the high, intermontane country east of the Blues.

Northeastern Oregon is a region with internal coherence. Its communities have interacted and competed with one another since their founding. The Blues to the west and north and the Snake River to the east inhibited contact with the areas beyond. The dry lands to the south, in Malheur County, were distant and lightly settled and of little importance to the towns in the Grande Ronde, Wallowa, Powder River and Burnt River valleys.

Distance from population centers has relegated northeastern Oregon to relative obscurity, even within Oregon. The only historical discussions of the region are locally published county histories. Most of the information for this study was, therefore, gathered from primary sources: county courthouse records, early photographs and maps, business directories, newspapers, unpublished manuscripts and documents, and interviews. Each of the towns and abandoned townsites was inspected in order to get a sense of its past and present roles, not only in terms of regional economics, but also as a place to live and visit—in short, to achieve some understanding of these towns' importance to a relatively remote and inaccessible part of our nation.

Acknowledgments

DURING THE YEARS spent on this project I have become indebted to far more people than it is possible to acknowledge individually, so I mention only a few. Special thanks go to Harvey Bennett of Eastern Oregon State College, who enabled me to come to La Grande in the first place through his offer of a job. During the months that I explored the region, Edward T. Price, Jr. of the University of Oregon Geography Department asked me pivotal questions I could not answer, guiding me to places and topics I otherwise never would have approached. In those places, countless persons kindly and patiently answered my own interminable questions.

My inquiry was made easier by the courtesy and interest of those who provided access to the region's old photographs and maps. Staff members of the University of Oregon's Map Library and Oregon Collection, of the Walter M. Pierce Library at Eastern Oregon State College and of the Oregon Historical Society in Portland all willingly shared their fine collections. Ethel Chandler of Elgin kindly provided many photographs (two of which are included in this book). The invaluable Sanborn maps are reproduced here with permission of the Sanborn Map Company of Pelham, New York.

The tasks of map construction, photograph reproduction and typing take endless amounts of time, so I appreciate the help of Don Chambers, Glenn Thomas, Bob Hicks and Sandra Gibson at the University of California, Riverside. John Evans of La Grande was kind enough to read the manuscript and point out inconsistencies. Everett G. Smith, Jr., Phillip H. Dole and Samuel N. Dicken, all of the University of Oregon, also read the manuscript and offered their comments.

For publishing this study, thanks go to the Oregon Historical Society; to Thomas Vaughan, Executive Director, to Priscilla Knuth, Executive Editor, to Bruce Taylor Hamilton, Book Editor, to Tracy Ann Robinson, Assistant Editor, and to Colleen Campbell and Katie Omundson Koerper of the Publications Department. Portland artists Julia Suddaby and James Longstreth also contributed their talents to this volume.

Finally, a thousand thanks to my family, without whose long-term sympathy I might never have finished. It must have seemed an endless process to my parents, Harry and Shirley Bailey, as well as to my sisters who assisted me in this project, Marian as an editor and Ellen as artist-turned-cartographer.

Everyone involved in this publication has striven for accuracy. Whatever is inaccurate is quite unintentional and I accept full responsibility. No one can ever know everything about a place. I hope, though, that this study will add to an understanding of a beautiful part of Oregon and the significance of its rich collection of small towns.

Introduction

THAT THE SMALL TOWN has been important to the American landscape is unquestionable. It has influenced a cultural philosophy that shaped its inhabitants and, to a certain extent, the nation. Historically, it has housed a significant portion of the nation's population and provided important services to the surrounding rural area. Main street, along which a small town's business and social activity is centered, serves to concentrate these functions as they would never be in a larger city. As one of the clearest indicators of a small town's development, this street warrants special attention. An examination of its role and what has happened to both that role and the street through time helps to reveal the historical significance of small towns, their relationship to surrounding rural areas, and why, even today, small towns are important.

An analysis of the businesses and the buildings that house them reveals much about a town's history, its character and the nature of the surrounding area. Changes in the town's businesses through time indicate its stability, its growth, stagnation or retrenchment. The physical structure of the business area indicates the perceptions of the town's founders as well as those of its subsequent occupants. In most small towns the entire business district is generally located along main street.

The vitality of a town depends as much on its role as an assembler of people as on its ability to satisfy their material needs. People's paths intersect on main street, and certain collective activities occur here and nowhere else. A downtown's social events are just as telling as its economic development; the social significance is clarified by economic changes. In fact, at least for the outlying areas, the town's social function is its most important role; this supports the idea that, even today, small towns are extremely important in the social fabric of a rural area.

The history of small towns in northeastern Oregon, one of the nation's most rural areas, is of particular interest today, in light of recent population trends. In recent years it has become increasingly evident that big-city growth is slowing and, in many areas, small-town residency is on a corresponding upswing. For those wishing to relocate, northeastern Oregon's small towns are well prepared to receive new inhabitants. Planned and built nearly a century ago, many of these towns have the potential to comfortably support a much larger population than they now contain. This study examines the various processes through which this potential developed, the focus of development in each case being the central topic of this study—main street.

MAIN STREET

Settlement of Northeastern Oregon

I

THE DEVELOPMENT of small towns is closely related to that of the regions in which they are situated; their histories of settlement, growth and decline are intertwined. Many early towns were founded as speculative adventures, as gambles on the future prosperity of a newly settled region. It was only when the surrounding region was more densely settled and its possibilities more thoroughly evaluated that the visions of town founders were put to the test. Only time could confirm the necessity for each of the towns that had been started. Before examining the ways in which the towns developed it is necessary to reconstruct a picture of northeastern Oregon as it appeared before it was settled, for it was this appearance that determined the expectations of the early settlers.

Natural Setting

Northeastern Oregon is located in an intermontane region; forested mountain ranges rim the skyline in all directions (**fig. 1**). Early settlement was centered in three valleys: the Grande Ronde Valley, the Baker Valley and the Wallowa Valley. The Grande Ronde and Baker valleys are in the western part of the region, on the sharply uplifted eastern flanks of the Blue Mountains. The Wallowa Valley is in the eastern part of the region, 15 miles from the margin of the Grande Ronde Valley to the west. The Grande Ronde and Baker valleys are separated by a ridge that rises into a major mountain range, the Wallowas, which continue the division of the two valley systems eastward. High, steep and heavily glaciated in the Pleistocene Age, they are an imposing divide across which no road has ever been built.

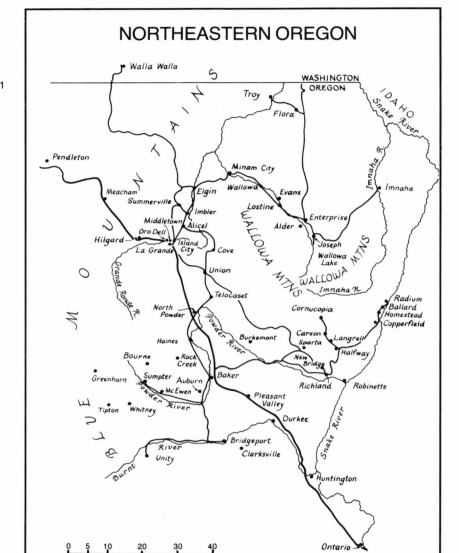

Fig. 1

NORTHEASTERN OREGON

2

The Baker Valley is the most southerly of the three principal valleys. Its floor, at about 3,300 feet in elevation, is traversed by the Powder River. The river rises in the Blue Mountains and flows east, on the southern side of the Wallowas, into the Snake River. The Grande Ronde Valley to the north is around 2,700 feet in elevation. It is watered by the Grande Ronde River, which, like the Powder River, begins in the Blues and flows into the Snake. However, after leaving the Grande Ronde Valley, the river becomes entrenched and unlike the Powder, has no space for cultivation downstream. Its largest tributary, the Wallowa River, does have an arable floodplain. This river heads in the Wallowas and flows west along their northern flanks to its junction with the Grande Ronde River. A racing stream, it drops in elevation from around 3,700 to 2,900 feet along its 15-mile length. The major clusters of settlement thus run east-west, along the valleys of the Powder, Grande Ronde and Wallowa rivers.

In addition, a fourth, smaller river has a collection of communities along it. The Burnt River Valley is one ridge south of the Baker Valley. This river, which also rises in the Blues and flows east into the Snake River, is considerably smaller than the others, its valley floor correspondingly narrower and its resident population smaller. It is primarily important as a transportation corridor in its lower reaches.

The climate and vegetation patterns of northeastern Oregon are fairly simple. The Blue Mountains crest at about 6,900 feet and the Wallowas at over 9,000 feet. Both ranges cause enough orographic rainfall to keep the sections close to them relatively wet. To the east and to the south, precipitation decreases with distance from the mountains. Temperatures, however, increase to the south, reducing the effectiveness of precipitation received; these areas are thus drier than might be expected. Within the region, the overall climatic pattern varies from place to place, locally modified by factors such as altitude or proximity to mountains. The result is larger climatic differences within the area than might be surmised from its seemingly minor individual statistical variations.

Regional vegetation patterns reflect the patterns of temperature and precipitation. The mountains are covered with forests

3

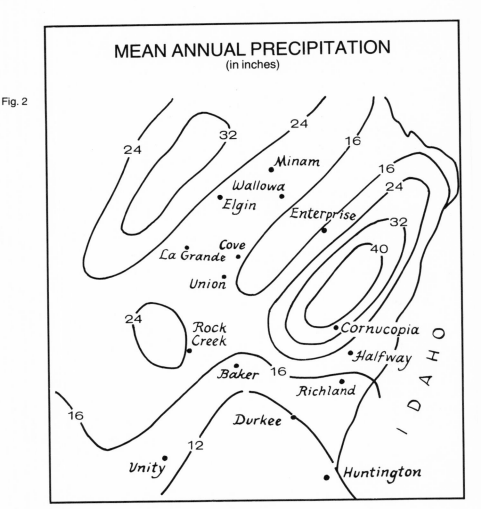

MEAN ANNUAL PRECIPITATION
(in inches)

Fig. 2

ranging from ponderosa pine at the lower treeline, at around 3-4,000 feet, to subalpine fir at the upper line, averaging 6,500 feet. The valleys are predominantly grassy. Northern Union and Wallowa counties, other than the mountains the coolest and wettest part of the region, have extensive pine forests on their upland plateaus and grasslands in their valleys. The transition to

4

the drier vegetation typical of the southern part of the region occurs entirely within the 25 miles between the northern and southern ends of the Grande Ronde Valley. At the northern end, pines extend onto the valley floor, then give way to grasses, which in turn give way to shrubs. Farther south, the Baker Valley is entirely grass and sage covered. In fact, Baker County's only forested areas occur at high elevations.

The early settlers correlated grass and forest with arable land, and sage with problems. The grassy valleys were settled first and then the forests were cleared for fields. The sage country was left to the stockmen. This basic pattern has persisted, with some shifts. Much of the forested land is no longer cultivated but has been converted to hay as farmers found the growing season short and cool. Some of the lower sage country has been irrigated and the higher sage country has been dry farmed. Dry farming in sage country has declined, however, and use of the land has reverted to stockmen.

Indians

As they entered the region, early explorers and settlers encountered many Indian tribes. Shoshone, Cayuse, Walla Walla and Nez Perce all traveled frequently through northeastern Oregon. While there was some hostility and armed conflict between them, the relationship between white settlers and Indians was generally amicable. The Nez Perce was the only tribe with strong territorial claims to the region, particularly to the Wallowa Valley. Under the guidance of Chief Joseph the Younger, the tribe fought to retain the Wallowa Valley but was eventually defeated and removed to a reservation in Washington state. (Chief Joseph last visited Wallowa County in 1902.)

Exploration

Northeastern Oregon was traversed by a number of explorers in the first half of the nineteenth century. Lewis and Clark passed to the north, but most subsequent parties traversed it (**fig. 3**). Among the parties were those of Wilson Price Hunt in 1811,

5

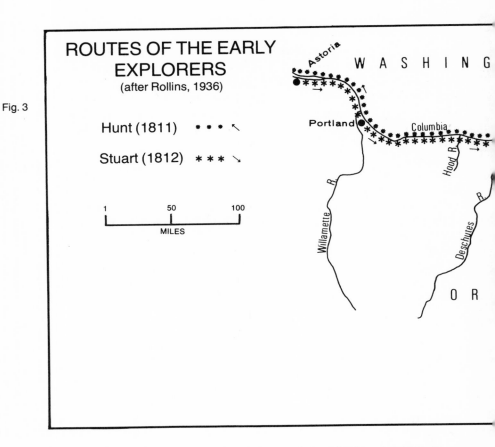

Fig. 3

ROUTES OF THE EARLY
EXPLORERS
(after Rollins, 1936)

Hunt (1811)   • • • ⌐

Stuart (1812)   * * * ⌐

1   50   100
|_____|_____|
MILES

Robert Stuart in 1812, Nathaniel Wyeth in 1832 and 1834, Benjamin Louis Bonneville in 1834 and John C. Frémont in 1843. Frémont's expedition was the last before the major settling migrations began. The journals of these explorers provide a glimpse of the area before settlement. Many of the difficulties they experienced were duplicated by the pioneers who followed.

The first white explorers to travel through northeastern Oregon were Wilson Price Hunt and his party in the winter of 1811. They were engaged by John Jacob Astor to seek a land route between the Missouri River and Astor's fur depot at Astoria, Oregon. Hunt and his party approached Oregon from the

6

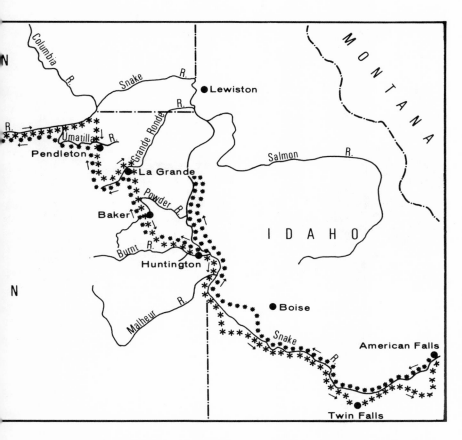

Snake River Basin. They tried at first to continue walking down the Snake River, entering Hells Canyon in early December. Difficult footing in deep snow on the steep canyon walls and lack of food forced them to retrace their steps to an Indian encampment.[1] There they learned that the route was considered impassable, but were told of a good trail leading through several valleys and over a mountain range. This they followed and so became the first white men to cross the Baker and Grande Ronde valleys.

In 1812, Robert Stuart led an expedition from Astoria eastward and closely approximated Hunt's route. With only minor divergences, the route Stuart selected developed into the Ore-

7

Fig. 4

The Grande Ronde Valley floor near Union, looking west. In 1843 Frémont stood at the crest of the mountain at the left of this photograph and looked across the valley. As he predicted, the valley proved attractive to farmers and by 1900 it was densely settled. (B. R. Bailey)

gon Trail. Both Hunt and Stuart had to depend on wild game for food. Also, they had to rely on local Indians to supply them with horses (used for transportation and food) and advice as to route. Indeed, although they may have seemed just as inclined to steal from a traveler's camp as to supply information and horses, these Indians were vital to the survival and success of the early explorers.

John C. Frémont's expedition of 1843 passed through northeastern Oregon over much the same route as Hunt and Stuart. Frémont was the last explorer to describe the area before the onslaught of traffic along the Oregon Trail heading for the Willamette Valley commenced. Actually, the migration had already begun and Frémont followed a badly worn and rutted road for the most part. Like his predecessors, Frémont started out from the Snake and traveled up the valley of the Burnt River, where he commented on the precipitous hillsides, ravine-like character of the valley and dangerously narrow and rough road. Nevertheless, he delighted in its greenness, so refreshing after the trip down the dry Snake River Valley. Standing on the summit of a hill east of the present site of Baker, he admired the grand panorama of the Elkhorns to his left, black with pines, and wrote that "descending from the summit, we enjoyed a picturesque view of high rocky mountains on the right, illuminated by the setting sun."[2] He was seeing the Wallowas, a magnificent sight.

Frémont found the country of the Baker Valley to be "constantly more pleasant and interesting" as he proceeded northward and spent the night near what is today Haines. The soil looked deep, black and fertile. The next day, October 17, 1843, he reached the dividing ridge between the Baker and Grande Ronde valleys and, looking over the Grande Ronde, paused to observe

a beautiful level basin, or mountain valley, covered with good grass, on a rich soil, abundantly watered, and surrounded by high and well-timbered mountains; and its name descriptive of its form—the great circle. It is a place—one of the few we have seen in our journey so far—where a farmer would delight to establish himself, if he were content to live in the seclusion which it imposes. It is about 20 miles in diameter; and may, in time, form a superb county.[3]

Frémont then proceeded through the valley and, rather than climb the steep ridge west of present La Grande as the early emigrant road did, he decided to find another way over the Blue Mountains. Consequently he continued north across the valley, cutting through Pumpkin Ridge along the short gorge of the Grande Ronde River, and emerged in what is today called Indian Valley, where Elgin lies. He commented that

the trail conducted into the open valley of the stream—a handsome place for farms; the soil even of the hills, being rich and black. Passing through a point of pines, which bore evidences of being much frequented by the Indians, and in which the trees were sometimes apparently 200 feet high and 3 to 7 feet in diameter, we halted for a few minutes in the afternoon at the foot of the Blue Mountains.[4]

9

Early Settlement

Many groups participated in the settlement of the West. Frederick Jackson Turner's theory of frontier settlement* can be applied to northeastern Oregon, although the sequence was not as neat as his model suggests. Nonetheless, comparison of Turner's theory to the actual situation shows that northeastern Oregon was clearly a full-fledged participant in the Western experience so often identified with more legendary parts of the country.

Turner's succession of settlement can be summarized as follows. Explorers described parts of the frontier in published accounts that were widely read. In many cases, the first non-Indian people to appear in an area were fur traders and trappers. They set up semi-permanent camps to which Indians brought furs for trade. Roaming cattlemen, another group to initially occupy areas of the West, drove their herds across the open range, eventually to market. During this time every eye was peeled for the glint of gold, and once a site was suspected miners came rushing to the new area. Miners often established a region's first settlements as they clustered in the vicinity of gold strikes. Their camps appeared as if from nowhere, and the exorbitant prices they paid for food and supplies were well known. The presence of large numbers of hungry, free-spending miners encouraged farmers to settle nearby, for they could count on a ready market for their products. Farming populations needed their own supplies and so towns were founded by merchants who served the farmers, miners and passing traffic.

In northeastern Oregon, fur traders were active for many years before any permanent settlers arrived. They may even have maintained fairly permanent camps. Hunt and Stuart both were engaged by John Jacob Astor's Northwest Fur Company to seek a land route from Oregon to Missouri. Their journals of 1811 and 1812 contain numerous observations regarding animal populations and the pelts the Indians presented to trade.

---

*This theory was first espoused in "The Significance of the Frontier in American History," a lecture presented in 1893, later published in Turner's *The Frontier in American History*, New York, 1920.

Fig. 5

Sparta, looking east. The rolling terrain is typical of the upland of the Blue Mountains and the Wallowas' southern flanks. (B. R. Bailey)

When Frémont toured the area 30 years later, he commented that the fur-bearing animals had been hunted out. Even so, the Hudson's Bay Company maintained a camp in the Grande Ronde Valley, probably as late as the early 1860s.[5]

Cattleman, miner, pioneer farmer and merchant all began to arrive in northeastern Oregon between the winters of 1861 and 1862. The cattlemen, a transient lot, are hard to place and date but Oregon historian Lewis A. McArthur locates them in the eastern part of the Powder River drainage, locally called Eagle Creek, in early 1861.[6] Next came the miners, who arrived soon after gold was discovered in the foothills of the Blue Mountains in October, 1861. Placer deposits attracted thousands of prospectors who were soon served by the first town in the region, Auburn, a mining camp that boomed early in the decade.

The local gold rush also attracted merchants and farmers. The first settlers to winter over in the Grande Ronde Valley in 1861 did so in direct response to the boom to the south. Two

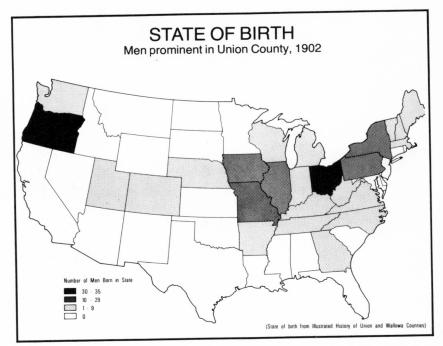

STATE OF BIRTH
Men prominent in Union County, 1902

Fig. 6

Number of Men Born in State
- 30 - 35
- 10 - 29
- 1 - 9
- 0

(State of birth from Illustrated History of Union and Wallowa Counties)

small entrepreneurs and a disgruntled family moving away from Walla Walla settled in the Grande Ronde Valley planning to establish a freight route to carry supplies from the Columbia River to the mining area. The following year these first settlers raised hay for sale to passing traffic and ran a small inn for travelers.[7] In the summer of 1862 they were joined by others who established farms and ran cattle on the valley floor. Eventually miners built homes in the Grande Ronde Valley as a base for their families while they went off to mine. Within a year of the valley's initial settlement several small communities developed, which were eventually platted and became important towns.

Origins of Settlers

Within 20 years of northeastern Oregon's initial settlement, all good land in the valley floors had been homesteaded and a num-

12

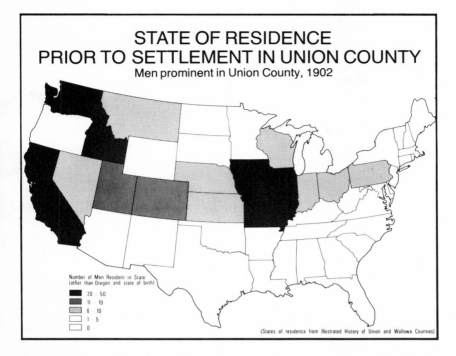

STATE OF RESIDENCE
PRIOR TO SETTLEMENT IN UNION COUNTY
Men prominent in Union County, 1902

Fig. 7

Number of Men Resident in State
(other than Oregon and state of birth)
20 - 50
11 - 19
6 - 10
1 - 5
0

(States of residence from Illustrated History of Union and Wallowa Counties)

ber of towns had been founded. Settlers created a tidy landscape. The nature of these places in part reflects the settlers'
preconceptions of what towns, farms and landscapes should
look like, in other words, the settlers' origins.

A Union County history published in 1902 includes the biographies of over 250 prominent county residents.[8] Sifting
through the volume, one finds that nearly all the men were born
in the Northeast and Midwest, from New York and Pennsylvania
to Missouri and Iowa (see **fig. 6**). This was a region with numerous small towns embedded in a landscape of mixed farming.

The movement of the men after leaving their home state is
also interesting (see **fig. 7**). Many of them came west gradually,
moving several times before they crossed the Great Plains. Often
this was in childhood as their parents relocated westward. A
large number went west as the proverbial single young man
seeking his fortune. Most of them went to mine and stopped in

13

such states as California, Nevada, Colorado, Montana and Idaho, usually in the mining districts, often in towns that no longer exist. Two other states stand out as important destinations. One was Utah, which, being Mormon, had a specialized appeal (the Mormon influence eventually extended to northeastern Oregon and is still visible on the land).* The other state was Washington. Usually the young men logged around Puget Sound or Fort Vancouver, or tried their hand at wheat ranching around Walla Walla.

Men came to Union County for diverse reasons. Some first traveled through the area as teamsters, hauling supplies from the Columbia to mining districts in Baker County and farther east in Idaho. Some came as miners who eventually drifted into Union County. Others, down on their luck, simply came to join a relative who had already settled in the county. And there were even those who had started out farming in the Willamette Valley but shifted east.

Generally, the women who moved west to Union County had a less adventurous journey. Most of them came with their parents and families. Since the published biographies are limited to wives of prominent men, it is impossible to know about the travels of unattached females. Some women managed to get west on their own, however. During the covered wagon days, the basic wagon unit was the family, so the single travelers did not have the privilege of riding in a wagon. They were, however, permitted to join the wagon train as pedestrians if they contributed labor in return for the security of membership in the wagon party. Several women who rose to prominence in Union County walked across the plains with a wagon train, serving as the bakers

---

*An interesting illustration of this influence is the community of Nibley, east of La Grande and near Cove. In a sense Nibley was a corporation community, somewhat like either a logging or railroad construction camp. The town was established in 1898 as a base for Mormon field workers who worked on a Mormon corporation sugar beet farm. Within five years it had about 25 houses and a church but sugar beet yields were poor and the corporation and community both failed. Unplatted, Nibley never developed enough of a business district to ever fall within the definition of a town proper.

for the group. One travel account describes how many sturdy pairs of shoes were worn out on the walk.[9]

Settlement Expansion Within the Region

Northeastern Oregon's earliest settlers settled in the Baker and Grande Ronde valleys. Their arrival in the region was relatively late, but once settlement began it proceeded quickly. Within 20 years the most distant corners of the region had been investigated and evaluated as to their potential for settlement. The two principal valleys retained their dominance, however, with the highest rural and town populations. The Wallowa Valley was settled 15 years after its western neighbor and eventually became a population center itself, although considerably smaller. When county boundaries were finally stabilized, each valley formed the core of a county with the Wallowa Mountains marking the boundary between Baker County to the south, Union County to the northwest and Wallowa County to the northeast (see **figs. 1, 8**).

The three counties, each with distinctive physical environments, provided the early settlers with choices for supporting themselves. They fanned out to farm, raise cattle, mine gold and, later, to cut timber. The region's limitations, however, were less obvious and could only be identified through time. Some places were too dry to farm without irrigation, some were too cold for the wintering of cattle, some had a growing season too short and cool to ripen the fruit in the newly planted orchards. Settlement expansion outward from the Grande Ronde and Baker valleys can be traced in census statistics for population and agriculture (**tables 1-4**). With these statistics, the subsequent adjustment to regional limitations can also be followed.

The census information presented here is manipulated from the way it appears as originally published. In the years since northeastern Oregon's initial settlement, several county boundaries have been changed, involving the administrative transfer of hundreds of people from one county to another. In addition,

15

census district boundaries within the counties have been changed.

The county boundary changes resulted from the creation of new counties out of old ones and later boundary adjustments. Briefly summarized, Baker County was created from Wasco County in 1862 and, in 1864, Union County was created from Baker. Thus, both Baker and Union counties first appear in the census of 1870 and again, intact, in the census of 1880. In 1887, Wallowa County was created from the eastern portion of Union County, taking with it nearly a quarter of the latter's population. Also in 1887, Malheur County was formed from the southern part of Baker County, reducing that county's population. Then in the 1890s, a small area was transferred from Union to Wallowa County. Finally, in 1902, Union County lost its last eastern section when its "panhandle" was transferred to Baker County. The panhandle contained nine precincts and 2,700 people. It was an important area and included the mining districts of Sparta, Cornucopia and Iron Dyke, and two major agricultural valleys, Eagle and Pine.

By adjusting the statistics from the censuses of 1870, 1880, 1890 and 1900 to conform to present-day county boundaries, an entirely different pattern of regional growth emerges from that indicated by the figures as they were originally assigned. Throughout the following discussion, the settlement of the counties is described using their modern boundaries. Thus, for example, although settlement of the panhandle section took place while it was part of Union County, and it was an important element in Union County affairs at the time, its settlement is discussed here as part of Baker County.

A more complicated reevaluation of census statistics was necessitated by the major census district boundary changes that began in the 1950s. Census districts before 1960 were usually county election precincts, locally designated. Generally, each district was centered around a community and represented a cluster of population, probably in a valley or on a sliver of plateau. As counties redistricted, their census district boundaries shifted, and some new precincts were created while others were eliminated. In 1960, the census districts were completely re-

CENSUS DIVISIONS, 1970

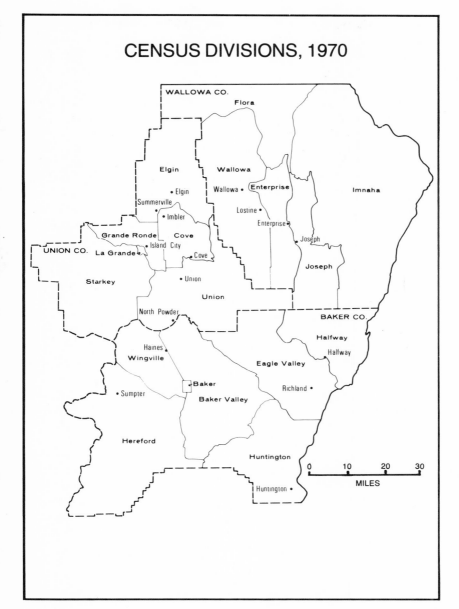

Fig. 8

17

vised. For the first time, the districts were defined by the United States Census Bureau. They were designed to follow major natural features and also to delimit the trade area of the principal town within each unit. Many smaller districts were combined into a few larger ones.

Census divisions were again slightly redrawn between 1970 and 1980. In Baker County, Baker and Baker Valley divisions were merged and the other divisions slightly modified. In Union County, the Grande Ronde division was dropped, essentially having been consolidated with the La Grande division. The county's remaining divisions were also slightly readjusted. In Wallowa County, all of the divisions were slightly redrawn except for Flora.

In spite of these changes, by comparing maps of the old and new census districts, and keeping in mind where the population nodes were, it is possible to correlate the nearly 90 old districts with the 16 that exist in the 1980s (see **tables 1-3**). The accuracy of the correlations is confirmed by the way in which the combination of old districts in 1950 add up nearly to the same numbers given for 1960, when the major division occurred. If an old district has been assigned to a wrong new district, a sizable discontinuity in numbers occurs, both in the district to which it was incorrectly assigned and in the district in which it should have been included.

In the rural parts of the counties, there is less problem in transferring census district systems: the old districts combine very neatly into the new ones. However, the old census districts associated with several towns pose problems. In Wallowa County, Enterprise and Joseph extended their town precincts up to 20 miles into the country. With boundary juggling, sections of the towns were shifted from one old district to another, some even shifted across new census boundaries, obscuring the distinctions between Enterprise and Joseph. In some situations it is helpful to combine these two towns and consider them a single unit. The city of Baker poses similar problems. The precincts around it were particularly unstable, in both their names and boundaries, making consistent comparisons for the districts of Baker, Baker Valley and Wingville difficult.

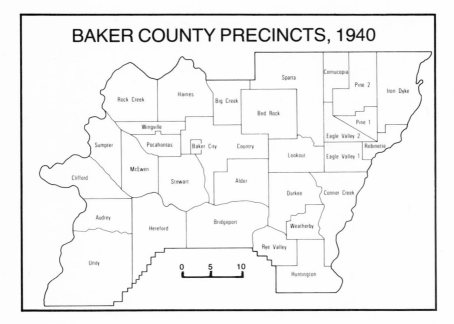

BAKER COUNTY PRECINCTS, 1940

Fig. 9

Sparta
Cornucopia
Pine 2
Iron Dyke
Rock Creek
Haines
Big Creek
Bed Rock
Pine 1
Wingville
Eagle Valley 2
Sumpter
Pocahontas
Baker City
Country
Robinette
Lookout
Eagle Valley 1
McEwen
Clifford
Stewart
Alder
Durkee
Conner Creek
Audrey
Bridgeport
Weatherby
Hereford
Rye Valley
Unity
0   5   10
Huntington

Baker County

Baker County (**fig. 9**) is the driest county in northeastern Oregon. Its valley floors are grassy and its hills shrub covered. Only the mountains support forests. Early settlers selected the valley floors for their farms and left the sage country to stockmen. The forests were of little economic use except for local construction until the 1880s, when construction of the railroad in the region made lumber export possible. Still the mountains were the scene of much activity for prospectors and miners. The balance of activity in Baker County shifted among farming, stockraising, logging and mining.

Mining was actually the area's first important activity, and as such responsible for putting northeastern Oregon on the map. Placer gold deposits were discovered in 1861 in a stream draining from the Elkhorn Mountains, the local range of the Blue Mountains rising above Baker Valley. Thousands of men swarmed into the Elkhorns seeking gold. Northeastern Oregon's first post office opened in the mining camp of Auburn, the first town in the region, established in 1862. The census schedule of 1870 reveals that nearly half of the men in the county were miners and that a third of all the residents were Chinese, most of whom were miners (although there were a few Chinese merchants, laundry men, professional gamblers and prostitutes). The miners worked the placer deposits either in the foothills of the Elkhorns or to the southeast, along the valley of the Burnt River in the Bridgeport district where the short-lived towns of Bridgeport and Clarksville were established in 1862. Baker Valley, on the other hand, was populated by farmers and their families. Baker City was platted in 1864 in the valley but grew slowly at first. The sage-covered hills above the Burnt River supported cattle tended by itinerant stockmen. The dry eastern parts of Baker County were sparsely occupied by farmers and stockmen.

By 1880, the placer deposits had been worked out and the miners had dispersed. New mining districts had opened to the east in the Sparta district, centered around the town of Sparta (established in 1872) on the southern slope of the Wallowas, and to the southeast in the Conner Creek district, along the Snake River. In addition, fresh placer deposits had been located farther upstream in the Elkhorns, in the Cracker Creek district. The semiarid Eagle Valley, below Sparta, now had several hundred people in it and the hills above the valley were well grazed. The city of Baker grew rapidly and included nearly a third of Baker County's total population.

The 1880s saw rapid growth in the smaller drier valleys of Baker County as these areas were homesteaded and irrigation ditches constructed. Eagle Valley continued to develop and farther east, the higher, cooler and wetter Pine Valley showed dramatic growth. To the south, the dry valleys along the Burnt River experienced a significant influx in the areas of Hereford and Durkee (called Express at the time). New mining districts also fostered growth in some parts of the county. Above Pine Valley, fairly high in the Wallowas, where the Cornucopia district mines opened, the town of Cornucopia was platted in 1886. Just to the east of Baker, the Virtue mining district was opened. Rural populations continued to grow in the southern, lusher end of the Baker Valley in the section known as Wingville.

The 10-year period from 1880 to 1890 also saw construction of the Oregon Railway and Navigation Company line from Portland to Salt Lake City through Baker County and the platting of Haines and Huntington along the new line in 1886. Several local spur railroads were subsequently built. The Sumpter Valley Railway was built from Baker to the Cracker Creek mining district and then over the mountains to Prairie City. This wood-burning railroad was basically for logging although it did maintain daily passenger service, one train a day in each direction. It was important in mining operations as well because it permitted shipment of ore to smelters in Tacoma and Salt Lake City. Once ore processing became a possibility, interest in the Cracker Creek district increased and the town of Sumpter was platted there in 1889. McEwen was platted midway between Baker and Sumpter in 1891. Work on a second spur, the Northwest Railway, commenced down the Snake River from Huntington with the goal of reaching Lewiston, Idaho. The tracks never reached Lewiston but did improve access to the Eagle and Pine valleys, with passenger service scheduled several times a week to the end of the line at Homestead, several miles below the junction of Pine Creek and the Snake River.

The last decade of the nineteenth century was an interval during which Baker County's population doubled, reaching nearly 19,000 people, a level it has never reached since. Much of this dramatic growth was related to mining expansion and new strikes in the Elkhorn's Cracker Creek district. The dry eastern end of the county sustained rural growth associated with irrigation expansion. Richland was platted in 1897 in Eagle Valley. The populations of Pine Valley and Eagle Valley grew by nearly half, Cornucopia's doubled, and Carson, Pine Valley's first platted town, was platted in 1900. To the south, railroad stimulus nearly doubled the population of Huntington.

By 1910, the population of Baker County had stabilized, but in numbers only. Within the county there was quite a bit of shifting. The western end, which had boomed from 1890 to 1900, showed a serious decline. The Cracker Creek district, centered around Sumpter and Bourne (platted in 1902), and the Greenhorn district, centered around Greenhorn (platted in 1904), lost nearly two-thirds of their population. The logging communities

21

Fig. 10

HU NTINGTON - ORE.

Huntington, about 1900, looking southeast. The Snake River flows between the ridge forming the skyline and the lower hills in front of it. The
grass and shrub covered hills are typical of northeastern Oregon's southern and eastern sections. In 1900 Huntington was one of the region's
largest towns. A railroad center, its main street business district developed opposite the depot and hotel (left). As in all early towns, livery
stables adjoined the business district and homes and churches were widely spaced through the blocks. With its wide streets, bare front yards, and
few trees, turn-of-the-century Huntington had the stark appearance typical of new towns in dry areas. (OHS neg. 63325)

in the census districts of McEwen, Clifford and Audrey (including Whitney, platted in 1900, and Tipton, 1904) that had grown
along the Sumpter Valley Railway declined as well. The eastern
end of Baker County, however, was growing spectacularly. Construction of the Northwest Railway down the Snake River to
Lewiston was at its height and a large copper mine was opened in
the Iron Dyke district along the Snake. Five towns were platted
along the proposed route of the railroad down the Snake:
Copperfield (1907), Ballard (1907), Robinette (1908), Home-

stead (1909) and Radium (1913). Pine Valley and Eagle Valley continued to grow. In Pine Valley, Langrell was platted in 1906 and Halfway was established in 1907. In Eagle Valley, the old community of New Bridge was finally platted in 1908. Many new homesteads were taken out in the Bed Rock district, which stretched from high on a dry shoulder of the Wallowas down to the lower Powder River Valley. The town of Burkemont was platted in 1900 near a large deposit of copper ore in the Copper Butte district.

Along the southern margin of the county, the Burnt River gained population in its upper end, in the Unity and Hereford districts, but downstream, in the old placer mining section of Bridgeport, the population declined. Mining continued on a small scale above Rye Valley and Durkee, but these narrow, fertile valleys also supported dry farming and two new towns were platted here: Pleasant Valley in 1903 and Durkee in 1908. The railroad maintained some services at Durkee, enhancing its size. The Baker Valley district, which included the dry eastern and northern portions of Baker Valley as well as the Virtue mining district, was lightly settled and the decline of mining in the Virtue district reduced the population of the Baker Valley district to the sparsest in the entire county. The Wingville section, on the other hand, had grown substantially from 1890 to 1900 as an agricultural area, and in 1910 probably had the county's richest farms. Rock Creek was platted in 1903 in the district, to accommodate both the farmers and the miners exploring the Elkhorns to the west. All the while, the city of Baker continued to grow and house nearly a third of the county's population.

The census intervals after 1910 recorded gradual declines in most sections of Baker County. No new towns were platted after 1913. The city of Baker continued to grow, slowly, but the county population as a whole declined 19 percent from 1900 to 1970. The most dramatic declines from previous peaks occurred in former mining districts, but declines were also registered in rural sections. The Huntington section suffered a 59 percent drop from its high in 1900 and the Hereford district, which included the mining districts around Sumpter, dropped 82 percent from its high in 1900. Eagle Valley declined 61 percent

23

from its high in 1920 and the county's Halfway division (including agricultural and mining areas) dropped 53 percent from its peak in 1910. The one significant departure from this steady downward trend occurred in the Halfway division. Construction of two dams in the Snake River Canyon (Brownlee and Ox Bow) by the Idaho Power and Light Company in the late 1950s and early 1960s temporarily doubled the population of the Halfway division. Once construction was completed, however, the population of the district dropped again and by 1970 its population was less than it had been in 1950. Baker Valley's population has gradually decreased but redistricting renders specific statistical comparisons impossible. Only Wingville has shown any growth but as with Baker Valley, precision is impossible. It has shown a slight growth since 1960, probably as a result of the suburbanization effects of Baker.

Union County

Union County (as defined by its present boundaries) experienced a much simpler pattern of growth than that of Baker County. Basically, Union County (**fig. 11**) consists of the Grande Ronde Valley, parts of the surrounding mountain ranges and a small section south of the drainage divide between the Grande Ronde and Baker valleys. Union County is farther north than Baker County, and, less affected by the rainshadow of the Blue Mountains, it receives more precipitation, supports a lusher vegetation in its valleys, and has denser forests. The Grande Ronde Valley in particular is better watered than its counterpart to the south, Baker Valley, and has always supported a larger farming population. In Union County, the three principal activities have been farming, stockraising and logging. Stockmen in Union County have intermingled with farmers from the earliest settlement days and in the Grande Ronde Valley stock ranches have traditionally mixed with farms. Logging became an important activity with the arrival of the railroad and has remained so. In fact (unlike Baker County), most of the resident population in the Blues has been associated with logging activity rather than gold mining (little gold has ever been found in the Blues west of the Grande Ronde Valley). Each of the three major activities was

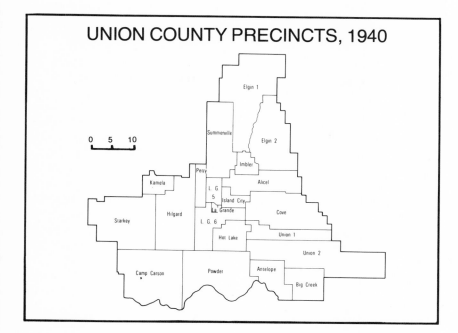

UNION COUNTY PRECINCTS, 1940

Fig. 11

Elgin 1

Summerville

Elgin 2

0   5   10

Imbler

Perry

Kamela

Alicel

L. G. 5

Island City

La Grande

Hilgard

Cove

Starkey

L. G. 6

Hot Lake

Union 1

Union 2

Camp Carson

Powder

Antelope

Big Creek

more intensive than in Baker County. Thus, although the land area of Union County is only 65 percent that of Baker County, Union County has been able to support virtually the same population.

The Grande Ronde Valley was the first part of Union County to be settled, although not all areas of the valley were equally attractive. In parts of its southern end the soil is highly alkaline, and before effective flood control was devised, large areas of the central valley floor were subject to spring flooding by the Grande Ronde River. Valley settlement began in the fall of 1861. By 1862, resident cattlemen were grazing their herds in the head-high grass; by 1870, with nearly all of the Grande Ronde Valley occupied, wild hay for the cattle was becoming scarce. The elevated eastern and western valley margins included in the Cove, Union and La Grande precincts were the most densely settled sections of the valley as early settlers avoided the swampy and alkaline conditions of the valley's central and southern portions. The towns of Union (1864), La Grande (1868), Oro Dell (1868)

25

and Cove (1873) were platted in an arc around the southern end of the valley.

Between 1870 and 1880, the settled area in Union County expanded to include nearly all sections of the county still occupied today. The productive northern end of the county, only lightly settled by 1870, grew substantially as settlers moved into the Summerville and Indian Valley districts. Summerville was platted in 1873. In 1874, Island City was platted along the road connecting Summerville and the Oregon Trail. Expansion continued far to the east into the Wallowa River Valley. In 1880, nearly a fifth of Union County's population resided in that valley, soon to become the center of the newly created Wallowa County. Settlement also extended to the south. To the southeast, settlement spread up Catherine Creek, over a low pass, and into the Park and Big Creek sections. The Park, a high mountain valley, skirts the Wallowas and drains into Big Creek and the Powder River. Also within the Powder River drainage, but farther west, Union County's Powder district was created as people settled this short-grass and shrub country that was actually an extension of Baker County's terrain.

The population of Union County doubled between 1880 and 1890. Much of this growth was absorbed in the county's many small towns but expansion also occurred in rural areas, particularly those which, because of their dry conditions or mountain locations, had not been settled earlier. The southern margin of the county continued to grow and a new district called Antelope, the driest in the county, was created between the districts of Big Creek and Powder. Antelope's growth was doubtless due in large part to the shortage of land available to homesteaders elsewhere. Settlement there was stimulated by the construction of the transcontinental railroad through Antelope and the establishment in 1885 of a small railroad community, Telocaset, at the crest of the grade between the Grande Ronde and Baker valleys. The new railroad also promoted growth in the Powder district; the town of North Powder was platted along it in 1885. Meanwhile, at the northern end of the county, Indian Valley and Summerville maintained the rapid growth rate of the previous decade. Indian Valley was now called the Elgin district, after the town of Elgin, which was platted there in 1886. In contrast, the

26

old agricultural section around Cove developed slowly and Island City actually lost population.

The Blues west of the Grande Ronde Valley were also settled during the 1880s. For many years miners had sought gold in the Camp Carson area (at the headwaters of the Grande Ronde River) with little success and by now their numbers were few. Homesteaders and cattle ranchers in the Starkey district, a relatively flat area typical of the upland surface of the Blues, were quick to move in when the area was opened to them. However, the largest influx into the Blues came during railroad construction. The railroad made possible the export of lumber produced by big logging operations and for the first time, the Blues were heavily logged. A railroad construction camp was converted to a logging camp at Hilgard (platted in 1888), and in the next 10 years another logging town was constructed several miles farther down the Grande Ronde River at Perry. The decade thus saw expansion into areas that had previously been only marginally settled; as it turned out, most of them were later largely abandoned.

The decade from 1890 to 1900 was relatively inactive in Union County in terms of population shifts. Growth in the northern end of the county continued and in fact peaked in 1900, after which the area's population declined, regaining the same size only in the 1970s. In the southern part of the county, the population in the arid districts of Antelope and Powder decreased slightly but Big Creek remained stable and the area around Union grew slightly. The Blues were also stable and the drop in the Hilgard mountain logging district was offset by growth in Perry. The homesteaders at Starkey and the miners at Camp Carson were still trying to make a living. The areas that showed real gains lay in the center of the Grande Ronde Valley, in the Alicel and Island City districts, and around the city of La Grande. Alicel (1890) and Imbler (1891) were both platted in the Alicel district. Middletown was platted midway between Island City and La Grande in 1894. The city of La Grande boomed after the construction of the railroad in 1884, and by 1900, with a population of 2,992 (still only half of Baker City's population), it had become the county's principal town.

The next decade, 1900 to 1910, was again a stagnant period in Union County. No new towns were platted after Middletown. La

27

Grande absorbed two-thirds of the county's population increase. Other than La Grande, only two areas continued to grow: the central section of the Grande Ronde Valley and the Powder district. In both cases local railroad activity and their resultant increased importance as shipping points probably were responsible. Population in the Blues dropped dramatically as logging and homesteading came to a virtual halt. The population shrank in both the Hilgard and Perry districts and in Starkey was reduced by half.

After 1910, the county's rural population experienced general decline, as a result of farm mechanization and consolidation. Only the city of La Grande recorded steady growth, although some districts experienced brief upward spurts as temporary logging communities were established. Palmer in 1920, Big Creek in 1930 and Starkey in 1940 all grew because of logging operations housed in portable company housing and served by small private logging railroads. With the advent of the logging truck, Elgin, La Grande and Union became the centers of Union County's timber industry. Thus, the wood products industry has continued as an important employer; its employees, however, no longer reside in logging communities of the Blue and Wallowa mountains.

Wallowa County

Wallowa County (**fig. 12**) is the highest and coolest of the three counties in northeastern Oregon. Its eastern section is fairly dry and grassy but otherwise the county is forested. It is also rather isolated, set apart by deep river canyons on the west, north and east and by the Wallowa Mountains on the south. Two routes provide access. From the west, a single, two-lane state highway and a spur rail line from Union County link Wallowa County with the rest of Oregon. Another state highway leads north into Lewiston, Idaho. Wallowa County was settled relatively late and rather sparsely. Union County cattlemen seeking new rangeland approached the county from the west in the 1870s and the county was created in 1887. It never experienced a period of booming growth; rather, its settlers filtered in to homestead and graze

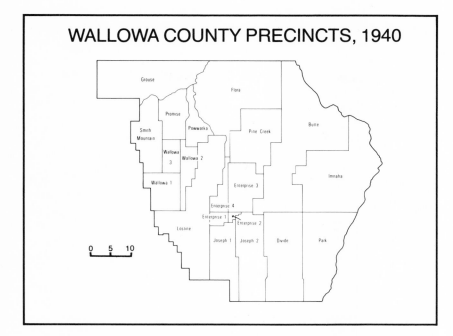

WALLOWA COUNTY PRECINCTS, 1940

Grouse

Flora

Promise

Smith Mountain

Powwatka

Pine Creek

Butte

Wallowa 3

Wallowa 2

Wallowa 1

Enterprise 3

Imnaha

Enterprise 4

Enterprise 1

Enterprise 2

Lostine

Joseph 1

Joseph 2

Divide

Park

0 5 10

Fig. 12

their extensive flocks of sheep and herds of cattle. The soil proved fertile, and the forests were gradually cleared. Wallowa County has developed as an agricultural county with logging an important secondary activity.

There are three sections of the county. Most populous is a band through its center along the Wallowa River and up onto the plain below Wallowa Lake. To the north, the Flora district spreads from the Wallowa Valley's grassy floor to rolling forested terrain. Lightly settled today, at one time it held nearly five times the present population. To the east is the dry and deeply dissected Imnaha district, whose few residents settled mainly along the Imnaha River.

The county's population patterns are easily described. The major precincts of the Wallowa Valley (Wallowa, Lostine, Enterprise and Joseph) grew until 1920 and then declined slightly. Each precinct included a platted town: Joseph (1883), Lostine (1884), Enterprise (1886) and Wallowa (1889). The town popu-

29

lations masked the county's sizable rural population, whose presence is indicated by the rural precincts of Leap and Prairie Creek.

Wallowa County's small towns served not only the people in the immediate valley but also provided the major services, including transportation, for the rural districts north of the valley. Many of these northern districts were close together as the crow flies but separated by the deep stream canyons near the gorge of the Grand Ronde River. Thus, although Powwatka and Promise were twice as far from Wallowa as they were from Flora the terrain directed their roads toward Wallowa. The rail line was completed to Joseph in 1908, and two more towns were platted next to it: Minam City in 1907 and Evans in 1910. The construction of the railroad consolidated the Wallowa Valley's importance as the county's commercial center.

The Flora district was first approached in 1878 by cattlemen who settled in the area of Paradise, and although Paradise proved to have severe winters, settlers persisted. The homesteaded precincts of Paradise, Lost Prairie, Flora and Mud Creek lay in close proximity on the south side of the Grande Ronde River. They were all served by the town of Flora, platted in 1897. The Grouse precinct on the high plateau north of the Grande Ronde River could be approached by ferry far below in the gorge, at the junction of the Wenaha and Grande Ronde. The town of Troy was platted in the gorge at the ferry site in 1910. The population of this northern area of the county peaked in 1910 and has since declined, although shifting logging activity brought new people into various sections temporarily. Despite the significant rural population decline, the land is still utilized, much of it having been consolidated into large wheat and cattle ranches.

The Imnaha division includes the precincts of Imnaha and Park, located along the Imnaha River, and the upland precincts of Divide, Pine Creek and Butte, located closer to Joseph, Enterprise and Flora. The only town in the district is Imnaha, established in 1902. Settlers in the Imnaha and Park precincts took advantage of the relatively low elevation and warm temperatures, planting orchards; residents of other areas of the county came to Imnaha each year to pick this produce for home canning. The steep grassy slopes of the Imnaha district near the Snake River, however, were devoted to sheep grazing. The upland precincts of Pine Creek and Butte to the north were cleared and dry farmed.

Logging has been an important activity in Wallowa County since the railroad reached it, and each of its towns had a large sawmill. Mobile logging camps briefly brought loggers into otherwise exclusively agricultural areas. The county's Smith Mountain precinct, for example, was created in 1920 because of a logging community. By 1930, when most of the loggers had left the area, the population had dropped by three-quarters; still, only half of the remainder listed on the census was classified as "rural farm." The nearby Maxville precinct, centered on the Maxville logging camp (owned by the Bowman-Hicks Lumber Company of La Grande), contained no recorded rural farm population at all.

Development of the various sections of Wallowa County was clearly differentiated. The Wallowa Valley contained a dense mixture of farms and towns. Population of the Flora section to the north was almost purely rural save for a few tiny towns whose residents totaled no more than 100. In fact, the county's outer precincts housed a more purely rural farm population than any other part of northeastern Oregon. In the United States census of 1930, Promise and Powwatka in the Wallowa division, Lost Prairie, Mud Creek and Paradise in the Flora division, and Pine Creek, Prairie Creek and Park in the Imnaha division had a cumulative population of 913 of which 897, or 98 percent, was classified as rural farm.

The Wallowa Valley has maintained its population while the outer precincts have lost theirs. In 1900, the Flora and Imnaha divisions, which combined held 28 percent of the county's population, were clearly important sections of the county. In 1970, they held only 7 percent of the county's population. Despite this decline, the rural areas of Wallowa County are still relatively important, with a higher rural:town population ratio than either Baker or Union County and agricultural activities have continued even in the most distant and remote districts.

31

Regional Economy

The regional economy of northeastern Oregon passed through several phases as the area was developed and exploited. Throughout its development, the three basic activities continued to be mining, logging and agriculture. Mining in Baker County stimulated initial growth of the region and continued as an important activity until after 1910. The early placer deposits and some of the later mines were worked as individual claims but the capital behind larger operations linked them with other far-flung mining adventures. Often, these larger mines were backed by English and Canadian capital. Funds from those sources were often divided between mining operations in northeastern Oregon and mines located elsewhere in the Northwest and Mexico. In 1911, Baker County mines were owned by individuals or corporations located in Philadelphia, New York and Chicago, in Lima, Ohio and in Fremont, Nebraska.* Distant ownership continued into the 1960s, as evidenced by the glossy folders about a Cracker Creek district mine prepared by a Vancouver, British Columbia mining firm seeking wider financing. At present, the only major operation mines limestone, manufactured into lime at the Oregon Portland Cement Company's plant in Lime, near Huntington; this lime has been used in major construction projects throughout the Northwest.

Railroads and logging have been closely linked in northeastern Oregon. The Oregon Railway and Navigation Company went as far as Huntington where it met the Oregon Short Line, which continued east across Idaho toward Salt Lake City. Large logging operations materialized after the railroad reached the region. The Sumpter Valley Railway, principally a logging railroad, was constructed in Baker County with Mormon backing from Utah. Its builders also owned the Grande Ronde Lumber Company, which operated a large mill and mill village at Perry,

---

*A group of Ohio people, headed by A.L. White, president of Lima Locomotive & Machine Co., owned the Baker County Greenhorn district's Ben Harrison mine. The Red Boy mine near Granite (also in Baker County) was owned by the president of Fremont Power Co. and his associates. "Mining in Eastern Oregon," *The Mining World*, 27 May 1911.

Fig. 13

Large-scale logging in northeastern Oregon became possible after the
Union Pacific connected the region with outside markets. To haul
trimmed logs out of the mountains down to their sawmills, logging companies constructed narrow-gauge railroads along drainages. Here
Sumpter Valley Railroad's wood-burning Climax Engine No. 3 waits
while loggers load the cars (at the moment, all hands have paused for the
picture-taking). (OHS neg. 52644)

near La Grande.[10] Small, narrow-gauge logging railroads were
built up around many of the region's river drainages. Their
grades and roadbeds are still visible although sections have been
obliterated by erosion or highway construction. Logging trucks
made the logging railroad obsolete, although the daily Union
Pacific run between Wallowa and Union counties is still used
primarily to haul board timber.

The railroad has continued to be a major employer in the region although its operation has changed significantly. With the
shift from steam to diesel and related subsequent decisions, the
roundhouses and shops in La Grande and Huntington were
closed and demolished. Passenger service to the area was discon-
tinued in 1970 and reestablished by Amtrak on an experimental

Fig. 14

Railroad roundhouse, Huntington (northeastern Oregon's other round-house was in La Grande). In these huge, circular buildings steam engine locomotives were maintained and repaired. This involved the region in a heavy industry of national scope, providing a town like Huntington with a regular payroll and a sense of purpose. With the switch to diesel engines and subsequent removal of the roundhouses, the region lost an important industrial role, and its sense of national involvement was drastically reduced. (OHS neg. 15902)

basis in 1977 (in 1927 there were eight passenger trains daily, four in each direction). The importance of the railroad in northeastern Oregon persists, however, as concretely illustrated by the impact of decisions, such as the relocation of division points, on the prosperity of the towns affected.

The wood products industry has also maintained its importance in the region. Almost half of northeastern Oregon is forested although not all of this land has commercial value. About 80 percent of the commercially valuable timber is in national forests.[11] In 1973, logging camps and contractors, sawmills and planing mills, veneer and plywood plants, and a particle-board plant together directly employed about 10 percent of the region's labor force and comprised its single largest manufacturing group.[12] The operations range in scale from large plants to one-person efforts. At the lower end of the scale, individually run logging operations or one- or two-man sawmills, are locally owned. The upper end, however, is controlled by nationally known companies such as Boise Cascade. The small private sawmills serve local needs, supplying fenceposts and gates, and rough-cut lumber for corrals and sheds. Plywood, veneer and finished lumber are mostly produced in the larger plants and exported from the region. Since the large lumber companies often base production decisions on national trends, the local economy is largely influenced by distant decision makers.

Farming and stockraising have been important activities throughout northeastern Oregon. Farms increased in numbers until about 1920 but, with subsequent consolidation, their numbers have declined and their average size has increased (**table 4**). Generally, land has not been abandoned although there have been changes in its use. Perhaps the greatest contrast between the farms of 1910 or 1920 and those of 1975, other than consolidation and mechanization, is the reduced numbers of sheep and dairy cattle. The Taylor Grazing Act of 1934, which put an end to unregulated grazing on public lands, immediately halved the number of sheep in the region. Beef cattle on the other hand have become increasingly important to the economy. Small grains comprise the major crop, of which wheat is the most extensively planted. The oat crop was once relatively important, partly because of its use as horsefeed, but mechanization has reduced this need. Acreages of small grain were most widespread in the early part of the twentieth century when there were relatively high numbers of sheep. With the switch to beef cattle, increased acreage has been devoted to growing feed, particularly necessary during the winter when the cattle are herded down from the national forest lands in advance of heavy snows. Another reason for the decline in small-grain acreage is the disappearance of the small, dry-farming homesteader who farmed in areas that are now less frequently cultivated or have been converted to rangeland.

Fig. 15

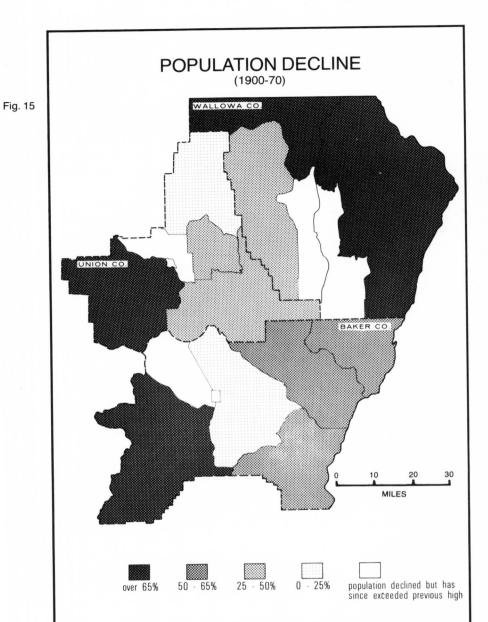

POPULATION DECLINE
(1900-70)

WALLOWA CO.

UNION CO.

BAKER CO.

```
0        10        20        30
|---------|---------|---------|
              MILES
```

over 65%   50 - 65%   25 - 50%   0 - 25%   population declined but has
                                               since exceeded previous high

36

The boom and decline of mining, the vagaries of the lumber industry, and farm consolidation, all have affected the population distribution of northeastern Oregon, generally by decreasing the population of the counties' more remote areas (**fig. 15**). The mining districts attracted a large number of mobile people. The districts and mining towns flourished but quickly depopulated when mining yields declined and the towns collapsed. In the early days of the wood industry, logging populations were located in numerous communities in the forested mountains. But as company sawmills were concentrated in the larger towns, outlying logging communities declined and disappeared. The reduction of mining and logging activity particularly affected Baker County's Hereford division.

The population decline in outlying areas was due primarily to low returns obtained by homesteaders and early farmers. Many of the areas produced only marginal yields which became less attractive as other types of employment (principally in lumber mills) became available in the region. Gradually, homesteaders sold out to neighbors, and those who stayed on found themselves increasingly isolated.[13] All of the outlying districts of the counties experienced significant declines in their populations. This depopulation of course affected the small towns that were located in these areas. The only districts whose populations have continued to increase are those located in the principal valley of their respective county and that hold the county seat. With the substantial decline in rural population, many districts in northeastern Oregon have returned to levels of occupancy typical of their early settlement.

37

Cornucopia

The
Founding of
Towns _____

II

A HISTORICAL ACCOUNT of town founding must initially address the matters of defining a town and dating its official beginning. The clearest demonstration that a town has been founded is the existence of a plat for it. A plat is the result of surveying the site and marking its streets, alleys, blocks and lots. The surveyor then draws a map, which is filed in the county courthouse. Existence of this map, or plat, is sufficient proof that a town has been founded; the day it is filed, the town officially assumes its existence. Though the site may never develop into what is usually considered a town, if a plat exists a town unquestionably has been founded. In northeastern Oregon 44 towns were platted.

Some additional sites developed that were never platted. Lacking this official record to document their founding, other identifying criteria must be adopted. One official act of recognition that can serve to locate and date a center is the establishment of a post office. In many cases post offices were established in rural communities years before they became towns, but since post office records provide the only unequivocal dates they are used here to date the founding. Not all post offices were associated with towns, however, so other qualifications must also be met. For the purposes of this discussion, an unplatted community is considered a town if it contained a post office, a store, a cluster of houses and several streets. In other words, it had to be a center with commercial and service functions, a resident population and something resembling the layout of a town.

The problem of defining an unplatted town arises only with respect to a few towns in northeastern Oregon which might be thought too small to be towns. Of the region's seven unplatted towns, five were fairly large; they grew and prospered without the sanction of platting. The other two, which were much smaller (housing at their peak population about 50 persons each), should be counted as towns because they were located in remote areas and so, despite their small size, functioned as important centers.

One group of unplatted communities is not included in the following discussion of towns: company-owned logging camps. These communities, self-contained and temporary, had little social or commercial interaction with their surrounding areas. The land, buildings and businesses were all owned by the lumber companies. Once the timber had been harvested from an area, the cabins were loaded up on company rail cars and hauled away. Logging communities, like railroad construction camps, were an extension of an industry. None of the unplatted logging communities developed into towns once the parent company withdrew support. Although interesting in their own right, these communities came and went with little lasting impact on the settlement of northeastern Oregon.

Towns were founded in northeastern Oregon between 1862 and 1915. Town founding did not always occur simultaneously with rural settlement. In the western sections, the earliest foundings did take place at about the same time as settlement but in the eastern sections, town founding lagged behind the rural settlement. Town founding is here divided into two periods: 1862-89 and 1890-1915. In the earlier period, towns were founded as the region was being settled. Their location was related to the early economy and transportation network.

By 1890, all sections of the region had been settled, some for more than 20 years. The second period of town founding revolved around northeastern Oregon's hinterland; towns were established in areas that, although settled for some time, contained no towns and were distant from any that were already established and developed. In some cases these hinterland towns were a byproduct of new railroad construction, established optimistically along the new tracks. In other cases, however, these rural locations simply reflected local sentiment that the area was sufficiently well populated to support a town.

The two periods of founding differed in important respects. The towns platted earlier were envisioned as large centers, containing many blocks and wide lots. The later towns were planned smaller, with few blocks and small lots; apparently their platters had more conservative expectations of growth—forecasts proved accurate by the towns' subsequent records of growth and survival.

The timing and immediate stimulus for town founding in northeastern Oregon varied but the towns ultimately all fulfilled the same role: they served as seats of commerce. The towns were places where goods and services were bought and sold. Local folk and traveler alike benefitted from the business and transportation connections towns provided. As centers of exchange, the towns were the intermediaries between local and distant producers. The establishment of towns greatly facilitated the provision of local needs and marketing of local products.

Pioneer Towns—1860-1889

The earliest pioneer towns (see **fig. 16** and **table 5**) were founded during the 1860s and early 1870s, and activity was renewed in the 1880s. During the pioneer period, towns were founded to satisfy one of two principal needs, either to service travelers or to supply local residents earning a living from the area's exploitable resources, and their sites were selected accordingly. Most of the travelers' service towns were situated at established resting spots (usually freighters' stations or stage stops), generally a day's travel apart. Although it was the region's settlers in need of supplies who ultimately provided the major support for these towns, the region's residential distribution did not directly determine the town locations. Generally these towns platted along roads were slow to grow, but enduring.

The second type of early pioneer town was quite different. It was located in the midst of a dense population, typically a mining community, service of which was its express function. Unlike the travelers' stops, main road location was not a requirement for founding. Often unplatted, this kind of town grew quickly, and disappeared quickly.

In the 1880s, railroad construction occasioned a spate of new towns. In their spacing, however, the new sites continued to cor-

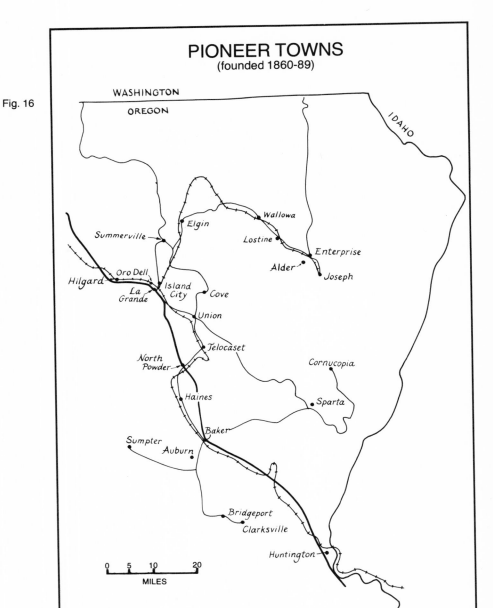

PIONEER TOWNS
(founded 1860-89)

Fig. 16

WASHINGTON
OREGON

IDAHO

Summerville

Elgin

Wallowa

Lostine

Enterprise

Alder

Joseph

Oro Dell

Hilgard

Island
City

La
Grande

Cove

Union

Telocaset

Cornucopia

North
Powder

Haines

Sparta

Baker

Sumpter

Auburn

Bridgeport

Clarksville

Huntington

0 5 10 20
MILES

42

respond to freight stations and stagecoach stops. A total of 24 towns was founded between 1860 and 1889, of which 15 have survived.

The principal road through the region was the Oregon Trail, along which traffic moved in the direction of its western terminus at The Dalles. By the 1860s, the great wagon migrations to the Willamette Valley had ceased. But the volume of traffic through northeastern Oregon picked up when gold was discovered in Baker County in 1861, and this resulted in the establishment of a number of gold-mining and road towns. During the pioneer period, five major mining districts were opened in Baker County, each of which generated at least one town before 1889. Of the six mining towns that developed, the first four (Auburn, Bridgeport, Clarksville and Sparta) were established quickly and were unplatted. By the time Cornucopia and Sumpter were established in the late 1880s, mining was dominated not by the independent prospector but by mining companies; accordingly, both these towns were platted by corporations.

Auburn is a classic example of a gold rush town. The community grew and declined quickly. Gold was discovered in the area in the fall of 1861 and miners began to arrive in large numbers in the fall of 1862. Lots were paced off and sold in some organized fashion but a plat was never filed in the county courthouse. In September of 1862, Auburn had about 200 houses and by November, contained over 1,000 houses and 60 stores.[14] Its prosperity lasted two years, and then mining yields decreased and the miners began to leave. By 1873, the town was down to 200 people after which the decline became more gradual. Auburn's post office closed in 1903 and now few physical traces of the town remain.

Despite its ephemeral existence, Auburn was a powerful factor in drawing attention to northeastern Oregon. The first town in the area, the region's first post office was established there, and the story of its gold attracted many people. It can be argued that the gold and the resultant town sparked the entire subsequent development of the region.

The other early mining towns were smaller but no less important in the region's growth, serving to draw people into the area. Miners comprised a large local market that encouraged farmers

Fig. 17

to settle in the region, hastening its agricultural development. Bridgeport and Clarksville, two small centers, provided a market for the farmers and cattlemen along the Burnt River. Similarly, Sparta purchased its food supplies from the farmers and cattlemen in the nearby Eagle Valley. In 1873, Sparta's population was (according to reports) about 300; in addition to other businesses, the town contained a general store, hotel, meat market and brewery, all of which depended somewhat on local suppliers.[15]

By the time Cornucopia and Sumpter were founded in the late 1880s, most of the nearby agricultural areas had already been settled. Cornucopia (**fig. 17**), located above Pine Valley, stimulated traffic in the eastern end of Baker County as well as encourag-

Cornucopia, looking south along main street, June 24, 1887, less than a year after it was platted. Although platters clearly indicated street widths, in reality early main streets' edges were poorly defined, with buildings irregularly placed, many set back unevenly from the street. The towns' owners, following the legalities of platting, always dedicated the streets to public use. The question of responsibility for building and maintaining the streets often took years to resolve, and in Cornucopia in 1887 the matter was still unsettled. Though most of this main street's buildings appear to be well cared for by their owners, the street itself was in poor repair. (OHS neg. 1641)

ing agricultural production within the valley. Sumpter, a small center platted in 1889, was a continuation of the mining tradition in the area and initially had little effect on the established town and economic patterns. About a decade later, however, it boomed, becoming the largest mining town in the history of northeastern Oregon. Located in the heart of the region's most productive district, a cluster of smaller mining towns grew up around it, which depended on it as a railhead and as a shopping, banking and service center.

Platted in 1864, Baker City was the first town to be established along the Oregon Trail in northeastern Oregon. Its early development was typical of the road towns, which, although located along a major road in order to serve travelers, depended for their survival on the growth of the surrounding areas. A photo-graph in the collection of the University of Oregon, probably taken in the mid-1860s, shows Baker initially to have been a ramshackle settlement with 19 unkempt buildings widely spaced along a dirt lane, surrounded by an unbroken sea of grass. However, with its centrally located, accessible site fairly near the main trace of the Oregon Trail, the town grew as the central supply depot for the mining districts to east and west. For nearly 60 years, Baker remained the largest, most important town of northeastern Oregon.

The other early towns founded along the Oregon Trail were in Union County. Union, La Grande and Oro Dell were all platted in the 1860s along the trail or one of its minor branches. A second road constructed over the Blues, the Ruckles Road, went to Walla Walla (which, in southeastern Washington, was the first major inland supply center relatively near northeastern Oregon). Summerville and Cove were platted along the Ruckles Road in the 1870s and Island City was platted on a local road connecting it with the Oregon Trail.

The settlement pattern that emerged in the late 1870s was a string of towns along the main through-roads and a scattering of mining towns some distance from the roads. The towns founded in the 1880s were also transportation based, except they were established along the new railroad. Telocaset, North Powder, Haines and Huntington were all established in 1885 and 1886 along the tracks of the Oregon Railway and Navigation Company (absorbed by the Union Pacific Railroad in 1890). All but Telocaset were platted, and in all cases the town site had previously been a stage stop. (With the railroad, this stage-stop spacing may seem anachronistic. However, since delivery of goods to the railroad still depended on horse-drawn transportation, it continued to be necessary that the distance between towns relate to the limitations of that form of travel.) Only Hilgard, a logging town platted in 1888 at a former railroad construction site, was located with greater regard to the exploitable resources around it than to its road access.

Wallowa County's towns were established in the 1880s, in locations chosen for reasons similar to those that determined Union County's. During that decade traffic crossed the county en route

Stage in Elgin. Towns once competed for stage and freight lines as they later competed for rail, air and bus service. Since stage lines linked towns with the rest of the nation, it was important to be on one. Centers of bustle and business, stage stops usually were located at a main street hotel. Here the stage, about to depart with a full passenger load, stands in front of the Hotel Elgin (also known as the Sommer Hotel) headquarters for the Joseph-Elgin Stage Co. (OHS neg. 63326)

to the mining districts of Idaho (which for a time provided a market for Wallowa County products). Traffic within the county was of small volume however, most of it locally generated. Joseph, Lostine, Enterprise and Wallowa depended primarily on local population for their support, serving as rural centers. A fifth town, Alder, established at the same time, was soon overshadowed by nearby Enterprise (which had been founded as the county seat). Wallowa County's population grew quickly enough in the 1880s to justify a new town in Union County on the intercounty road. This was Elgin, platted in 1886. Elgin (**fig. 18**) soon displaced Summerville as the largest town in the northern end of the Grande Ronde Valley, largely due to the decline of the Ruckles Road (which led to increased importance of the Wallowa

County connection) and to the desertion of Summerville's merchants to Elgin.

The towns founded in this period were either mining towns, towns established along important roads, or towns along railroads. All of these towns depended on the surrounding rural population for most of their business. The interdependence of mining towns and miners is clear. The towns along the road and railroads have a less obvious association with local farmers, for, as discussed, their sites were usually determined in reference to traffic through the region. Nevertheless, within a few years of their platting, they contained drugstores, general stores, hardware stores and flouring mills, all of which served the permanent resident rather than the traveler. Passing traffic supplemented these towns' economies, but did not constitute their base. Survival of the Wallowa Valley's towns, which were established along an only lightly traveled road, is an indication of the importance of the local economy as opposed to transient, imported activity. However, the bustle associated with the livery stables, railroad stations and hotels that serviced travelers certainly lent an air of activity and purpose to the road towns, increasing the impression of inevitable growth.

Hinterland Towns—1890-1915

The hinterland towns (see **fig. 19** and **table 6**) that were founded between 1890 and 1915 generally resembled those of the pioneer period. Continued mining activity and transportation developments stimulated further town founding. During the hinterland period, however, another kind of town also emerged: one whose primary purpose from the start was to serve the permanent rural population surrounding it—these were typically established in the more remote parts of their counties on roads that carried only local traffic. Twenty-seven towns were platted in this period, indicating continued enthusiasm for town founding. The only hint of more modest expectations for the region's development than those of the earlier period comes from the smaller size of the towns' initial plats. Of the 27 towns founded, only 6 have survived to the present; a discus-

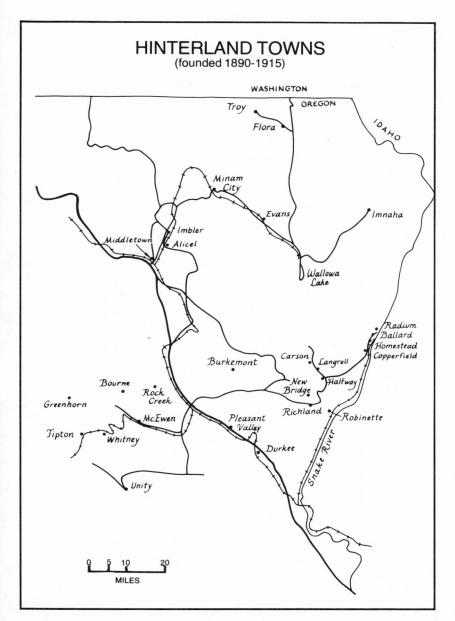

HINTERLAND TOWNS
(founded 1890-1915)

Fig. 19

WASHINGTON

OREGON

IDAHO

Troy

Flora

Minam
City

Evans

Imnaha

Imbler
Middletown Alicel

Wallowa
Lake

Radium
Ballard
Homestead
Copperfield

Burkemont

Carson

Langrell

Bourne

New
Bridge

Halfway

Greenhorn

Rock
Creek

Richland

Robinette

Tipton

McEwen

Pleasant
Valley

Whitney

Durkee

Snake River

Unity

0 5 10   20
MILES

49

sion of town founding during this period must therefore also include mention of subsequent failure.

The railroad continued to be the most important factor in determining a town's location, playing a similar role in this period to that of the mines in the preceding era. Railroads provided crucial access to the transportation of goods and people, created an atmosphere of excitement, drew settlers, and thus generated towns. As with mining, much of this excitement was short-lived. The towns founded along the railroad in this period were often situated in areas with too few people and an undeveloped economy. Because their survival depended on the productivity of the surrounding hinterlands or on their founders' enterprise, many of them failed.

Fifteen of the twenty-seven towns founded in this period were platted beside a railroad line, two of these along the main line of the Union Pacific and twelve more along the three new rail lines built after 1889. Only one of these lines still carries traffic: Union Pacific's spur line to Wallowa County out of La Grande. Four towns were platted along this spur. Three towns were platted beside the Sumpter Valley Railroad (which crossed the Blues to Prairie City) and five towns down the Snake River beside the Northwest Railway Company tracks. The last two rail companies failed as have the towns established along them.

To prosper, the towns founded along the railroads had to be supported by their hinterlands as well as being relatively free from competition with nearby communities. Those established along the Union Pacific spur line were in one of the region's most productive agricultural areas, but since that area was already being served by towns of the pioneer period, later town founders had to choose between less favorable locations along the line or enter into direct competition with the older centers. Alicel and Imbler, hinterland towns, were platted in the center of Union County's Grande Ronde Valley. Alicel soon faded but Imbler competed successfully against the declining Summerville to become the new rural service center for the valley's northern end. In Wallowa County, Minam City was platted in the gorge of the Wallowa River, near the old stage stop and river crossing. This location, however, lost its significance with the completion of the railroad and never developed. Evans, platted in the heart of the

Wallowa Valley, suffered from proximity to Lostine in one of the rare cases where the established road town retained its dominance over a new railroad town.

Pleasant Valley and Durkee, situated along the Union Pacific tracks in Baker County, were actually more characteristic of the towns established along the other two railroads' lines, for they were platted in less favorable areas; each was located in a small, dry-farmed valley traversed by the tracks. Pleasant Valley has disappeared but Durkee persists, as an example of a small town that has largely lost its economic base. Originally a stage stop called Express, by the mid-1860s Durkee was the only transfer point for the three stage companies that connected Umatilla and Walla Walla to the north with Boise and Placerville to the east.[16] Durkee also served a nearby small but steadily productive mining district. The community's well-being was later enhanced by its added role as watering stop and telegraph station for the railroad. The town was platted in 1908, near the time of peak population in the area. U.S. Highway 30, the first paved road in the region, passed through the town and a limited highway-oriented downtown business district developed. Now, however, trains no longer stop there and the new highway, I-84, bypasses Durkee. Its downtown business district is stranded and depends on the town's few residents and the surrounding rural population. Meanwhile, the freeway off-ramp has created another business district at a distance from the town and its old main street.

Of the towns platted along the Sumpter Valley Railroad and the Northwest Railway Company, those along the former had a more enduring hinterland economy. McEwen, Whitney and Tipton were established as logging towns. McEwen also served a small rural population but consisted of little more than a rail yard and general store. Whitney developed into a town with a small residential population and a small business district. Logging sustained the railroad until the 1940s after which time both Whitney and the railroad failed.

In 1898 the Northwest Railway Company started construction on a line that was planned to stretch from Huntington down the Snake River to Lewiston. The towns of Robinette, Copperfield and Homestead were platted in the canyon along the completed tracks; Ballard and Radium, platted farther along, coincided

51

with the proposed route but the line never reached them (and they were never built).

Each of the five towns was situated on one of the small alluvial fans built by the creeks that carve the canyon walls and drop into the Snake River. This string of towns illustrates several themes, indicating optimism about the development and growth that could be generated by railroad construction in an otherwise un-developed region, and representing the extension of the town network to the margins of northeastern Oregon.

The railroad and the towns along it did stimulate the development of eastern Baker County but neither the railroad nor any of the towns still exists. Copperfield originally typified the brawl-ing railroad construction camp but when construction halted, it quieted. Homestead persisted for some time, servicing miners working the copper deposits of the Iron Dyke Mine. In addition, as a railhead in an abundant orchard area, it shipped many boxes of fruit up the Snake destined for points east. Robinette was the nearest rail outlet for Cornucopia, Pine Valley and Eagle Valley and probably generated most of the freight hauled by the railroad. Ballard and Radium, the two towns beyond the end of the railroad, never developed as planned. Ballard remained Bal-lard's Landing, a ferry across the Snake to the Kleinschmidt Grade (a road out of the gorge to the Seven Devils mining district in Idaho). Freight traffic along the railroad, declining for several decades, finally ended abruptly in the early 1960s when rising water behind the new Brownlee Dam flooded the roadbed. Ro-binette and Copperfield were also submerged but the sites of Homestead, Ballard and Radium are still visible above the reser-voir behind Hells Canyon Dam.

Only three mining towns were platted after 1890, by which time the mining era was essentially over. The North American Mining Company surveyed Burkemont at a copper ore deposit in Baker County; the deposit was worked briefly but the town never developed. Greenhorn and Bourne, in the Blues, bela-tedly participated in the boom associated with Sumpter; they each briefly housed between 100 and 200 people but faded when the boom passed. Burkemont, Greenhorn and Bourne were the last mining towns founded in northeastern Oregon and their existence was ephemeral. Subsequent mining operations centered on the older mining towns of Cornucopia and Sumpter.

The unique towns of the hinterland period were the 10 founded as rural service centers. They were distinctive in their distance from rail lines and their location in agricultural areas, on secondary roads serving only the immediate vicinity. They were founded in outlying areas that had developed slowly and would peak in population about 10 years after the towns were platted. Generally, the district populations then declined, reducing support for these centers. (Most of these towns were located in the areas of northeastern Oregon that have since experienced the greatest population losses.)

Since 1890, the only towns founded that were planned exclusively as rural service centers and that have survived are Unity, Richland, Halfway, Langrell, Imnaha and Troy. The first four are in Baker County, and the latter two are in Wallowa County. All were founded almost 30 years after the first cattlemen occupied the valleys in which they are located, and each continues to serve a resident rural population, also benefiting somewhat from summer and fall recreationalists.

Unity in the Burnt River Valley (in Baker County's southwestern corner) was established in 1891 as a post office, and grew into a small unplatted town. With the opening of a large sawmill it acquired an additional service role, but when the mill closed the town reverted to its original function as a rural service center.

In eastern Baker County's Eagle Valley, Richland succeeded in replacing the older unplatted community of New Bridge, three miles away, as the principal service center. The area's first post office had opened in New Bridge in 1878, and that community had prospered by selling Eagle Valley agricultural products to miners from the Sparta district to the west; at one time New Bridge had a fruit and vegetable cannery, a box factory and a packing shed for the apples harvested from surrounding orchards. However, soon after Richland was platted in 1897 in response to the new mining and railroad activity along the Snake River to the east, New Bridge began to decline. Richland had quickly built a more elaborate and handsome business district than New Bridge, drawing away the latter's clients. Although New Bridge was belatedly platted in 1908, it never regained its former prominence.

Fig. 20

Imnaha, 1940s. Located in the dry eastern section of Wallowa County, Imnaha was established in 1901 to serve an isolated rural population mostly settled along the Imnaha River. In recent years the town has benefited from tourist travel to Hells Canyon through this remote part of Oregon. (OHS neg. 15926)

Pine Valley, northeast of Eagle Valley, contained four communities: Halfway, Langrell, Pine and Carson. Of these, only Halfway and Langrell became successful towns. The first post office, at Pine, was established in 1878 but Pine was never platted and did not develop. A few miles up the valley, a rural post office was established at Halfway's original site in 1887, but the post office was eventually relocated to the town's present site, which began to expand in 1908. Carson, platted in 1900 with only twelve lots in the entire town, was eventually overshadowed by the even smaller but more centrally located Langrell. Langrell, with only two platted blocks, is one of the smallest surviving towns in northeastern Oregon.

The towns in eastern Baker County were probably founded because of the stimulus of mining in Cornucopia and railroad construction down the Snake River from Huntington. The miners drawn into the region provided a local market and the railroad facilitated export of bulky agricultural products from the area, which, prior to construction of the railroad, had been isolated from the nearest rail shipping point (Baker) by long distances and steep grades.

Both Imnaha and Troy are along the margins of Wallowa County. Both were established to serve an isolated rural population and now benefit from summer and fall tourists. Imnaha's first post office was established in 1887 but the present townsite was established in 1901. The small unplatted community beside the Imnaha River (see **fig. 20**) falls marginally within the definition of a town used here. It is best known to tourists for its picturesque post office and as the last settlement on the perilous road to scenic Hat Point, overlooking Hells Canyon.

Laid out in the northern end of Wallowa County, deep in the gorge of the Grande Ronde River, Troy symbolizes the penetration of settlement into the more remote parts of northeastern Oregon. Troy sits at an old ferry crossing of the Grande Ronde, just downstream from that river's confluence with the Wenaha River. Even today it can only be reached by traveling unpaved roads, and it benefits from its remoteness. The town not only provides needed supplies to those ranchers who still live in the northern end of the county but also serves as the base for an outfit that organizes raft trips down the Grande Ronde and runs recreation pack trains into the Umatilla National Forest. Troy also supplies the many hunters who travel long distances every fall to hunt elk in the area.

Most of northeastern Oregon's rural service centers experienced a different cycle of development from that of the region's railroad and mining towns. While many of the latter developed into towns quickly and then failed, rural town growth was relatively slow and steady; once these communities developed into towns, they more often survived. Only three platted rural service centers became towns and then failed: New Bridge, Rock Creek and Flora. New Bridge, already discussed in conjunction with Richland (page 53), was platted in 1908 only after irreversible decline had set in. Rock Creek was surveyed and recorded in the Baker Valley in 1903, its development probably spurred by mining discoveries along the creek in the Elkhorns. But its proximity

Fig. 21

Parade in Flora, before 1910. One of the more remote towns in north-eastern Oregon, Flora, founded in 1897, was platted with large lots and wide streets (see fig. 22, facing). More than likely the group, with its abundance of flags, drums, guns and summer finery, was commemorating the Fourth of July. (OHS neg. 56814)

Right: Plat of Flora, recorded April 7, 1897. Although Flora, an agricultural service center in Wallowa County, was founded during the hinterland period, its plat is more typical of the region's pioneer towns, whose traditional characteristics include large lots, alleys, and standard street names. This town's small size, however, indicates it was platted later. (Wallowa County Deed Register)

to Haines and Baker (six and seventeen miles, respectively) apparently did not allow for successful long-term competition with these older, larger towns. Although in 1913 Rock Creek possessed several general stores and a butcher shop, all that remains today is a grange hall. The most substantial town to fail was Flora, platted in 1897 in northern Wallowa County (**fig. 21**). In 1910 it had about 200 residents and supported an eight-room school. But rural depopulation reduced support for its general stores, bank and newspaper, and eventually the town failed. Al-

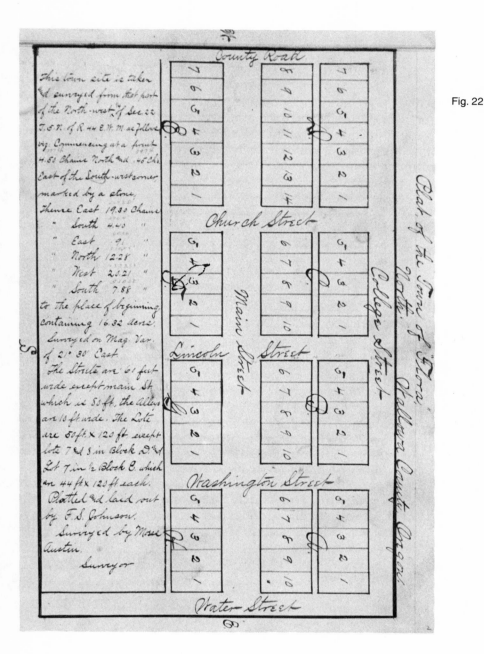

Fig. 22

though it still stands relatively intact, only a few houses have occupants.

Middletown, situated midway between La Grande and Island City, was an anomaly, perhaps best described as a precursor of future housing developments in the region. Platted in 1891 by the founder of Island City, it was not a typical town of the hinterland period, for the platted lots were five acres in size. Actually, Middletown could be considered the first suburban development in northeastern Oregon. Today a mobile home park occupies its site.

Plat Evolution Through the Pioneer and Hinterland Periods

In northeastern Oregon, towns were usually platted by people who had lived in the area for several years and who stayed on to promote the community and sell its lots, for which they received the returns. The evolution of town plats reflects the changing expectations of town founders; a plat's size indicates the founder's vision. In general, northeastern Oregon's earliest town founders were the most optimistic, planning relatively large towns shortly after the surrounding areas were settled, even if the local population was then only a few hundred people. Later platters tended to be more cautious. They waited until the region's population had increased and even then they platted small towns (see **figs. 22, 23**). Part of the reason for the increased caution and smaller plats is that a town's streets could not be built on or otherwise developed, one restriction of platting being that all streets and alleys had to be set aside for public usage and remain public regardless of whether the blocks and lots were sold or a town actually developed. This limited the uses of unsold lots or blocks. If the lots did not sell and the plat was vacated, the lots and streets were voided as legal units. In the meantime, however, the overly optimistic speculator was saddled with an undeveloped town.

In the pioneer period, towns were laid out according to fairly large and simple plans. A regular grid was typical of the early

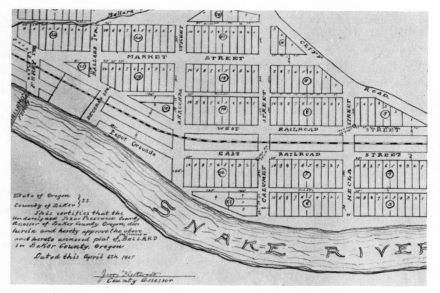

Fig. 23

Detail: Plat of Ballard, recorded April 6, 1907 (exactly one decade later than Flora, fig. 22). Ballard, in Baker County, was platted at a ferry point across the Snake River which served traffic to the Seven Devils mining district of Idaho. Its narrow lots are typical of the later towns platted in the region and the relatively exotic street names (which include Hecla, Calumet, Anaconda and Decoran) identify it as a town associated with mining. (Baker County Plat Book)

road towns, which ranged in size from 7 blocks (in Island City) to 25 (in Union) with their blocks evenly divided into simple lot patterns. Even larger were the railroad towns; their founders clearly anticipated important futures for them. North Powder, with 44 blocks, and Huntington, with 45, were planned as particularly sizable towns.

The mid-1880s saw the first variations in the standard plat, specifically the inclusion of town squares, and variation in lot sizes. Enterprise and Lostine were both platted with central squares. Enterprise's square became the county courthouse site, but in Lostine the square was kept vacant—it now serves as a sheep paddock.

59

The more widespread variation involved changes in lot dimensions. A standard lot, measuring about 50 by 100 or 60 by 120 feet, was compatible with the dimensions of the Victorian-style house (the typical architecture of that era), which could easily be placed on the lot with its narrow gable end facing the street and its long body trailing back through the lot. New lots introduced into some town plats halved this standard width. In downtowns these half-lots were later divided once more to make 12½ or 15 feet of street frontage, while in the residential areas, they were combined. A single residential property typically encompassed from two to four narrow lots. An exceptionally open pattern could result, with houses separated by wide vegetable and flower gardens.

Towns of the hinterland period were founded many years after the areas they occupied had been settled. In the western part of the region, Minam City, Alicel, Imbler, Middletown, Rock Creek, Pleasant Valley and Durkee were all platted in populated areas. Rock Creek, Pleasant Valley and Durkee, some of the smallest towns platted in northeastern Oregon, contained only two or three blocks. Their founders must have anticipated only modest growth.

The more remote towns were also small; perhaps the slow growth of the surrounding population cautioned their founders. Plats of Troy, Flora, Richland, New Bridge, Halfway, Langrell and Carson all contained eight or fewer blocks. Figure 21 conveys a sense of the size of Flora. In fact, the only exceptions to the small size of towns platted during this period were the railroad towns along the Snake River. Although their sites were restricted by terrain, these latter were nevertheless laid out with 10 or 20 blocks, subdivided into extremely narrow lots. Evidently, the railroad still appeared to be sufficient reason for a town to prosper.

Similar systems of street naming occurred throughout the region, with the familiar system of alphabetically and numerically named streets most commonly employed. Other towns used a set of presidential names or tree names. A few towns contained a Mill Street, College Street, Electric Street or Water Street, promoting local features or amenities (that may or may not have actually existed). Mining towns comprised the only group to use more unusual names; their streets went by the names of other nearby mining towns such as Auburn, Sumpter and Granite, and those of local mines such as Bonanza, Ibex and Columbia. These distinctive names may have served to link the towns together by association and to emphasize the glamour and gold; in any case they clearly set the mining towns apart from more placid agriculturally based settlements such as Richland and Flora with their Walnut, Vine and Church streets.

Summary

The history of northeastern Oregon's towns is linked with its regional development; evolution of the town network paralleled evolving settlement and transportation patterns. Parts of northeastern Oregon were endowed with a wide variety of natural resources that could be quickly and easily exploited, including fertile valley land, placer mineral deposits and rich forests. In addition, the western section was crossed by one of the major routes to the West Coast, the Oregon Trail. Once initiated, settlement in these areas proceeded rapidly and a number of small towns emerged. Settlement subsequently expanded into less choice areas with more difficult mining, shorter growing seasons, less rainfall, poorer soils, and especially, greater distance from markets. Although these outlying areas were occupied by settlers within a few years of the settlement of the principal valleys, their population growth was slower.

Settlement and town founding occurred in two phases. The pioneer period before 1890 was typified by rapid population growth in the more accessible and easily developed parts of the region. A skeletal network of towns was established. The construction of a transcontinental railroad through the region ensured that obstacles posed by distance from commercial centers would decrease.

After 1890, growth of the hinterland districts picked up in a fashion resembling the boom experienced by the initially developed areas. During this second wave of settlement, a new series of towns was established. This growth soon came to a halt, however, peaking at lower population levels than in the older sections. At the time they lost their momentum, these outer districts

61

were still too lightly populated to have achieved a self-sustaining economy and their towns were adversely affected.

The fundamental differences between the towns of the two periods have already been discussed in terms of town plats and locations. An equally significant difference between the two groups is seen in their survival rates. A total of 52 towns were founded, of which 23 survived. Of these 23 towns, 15 were founded in the earlier period and only 8 in the later period. Accessible location and hinterland prosperity, common to the earlier towns, proved advantageous. The later towns, mostly established in slowly growing districts, and lacking a foundation of local prosperity, proved to be poorly based. Many came to be little more than a plat in the county courthouse.

Those towns that have survived have in common two important characteristics: a good location and a dependable economic base. They are all situated along important roads connecting the principal agricultural districts with major highways, many have rail service, and all serve the surrounding rural area as well as a diversely employed resident population. Largest of the surviving towns are the centrally located county seats. The smallest are those at the other end of the connecting roads, in the more remote parts of their counties.

Those towns that failed (see **fig. 24**), failed predictably. Mining towns with worked-out deposits, railroad towns along railroad rights-of-way that were never completed or went out of business, logging towns surrounded by logged-out forests, rural towns in depopulated rural districts—all occur more than once in northeastern Oregon's history. In general, these towns grew up around a specialized economic activity, and when this base disappeared, so did they.

The fact that 52 towns were founded in northeastern Oregon is indicative of the high hopes shared by many of its early residents. Despite a high failure rate among towns from the very first, people continued to plat them, and in many cases, subsequent additions increased their size. Downtowns and main streets develop in part in relationship to the size of the towns they serve and the times in which they grow. Thus, before main street development can be understood, the nature of town growth should be examined.

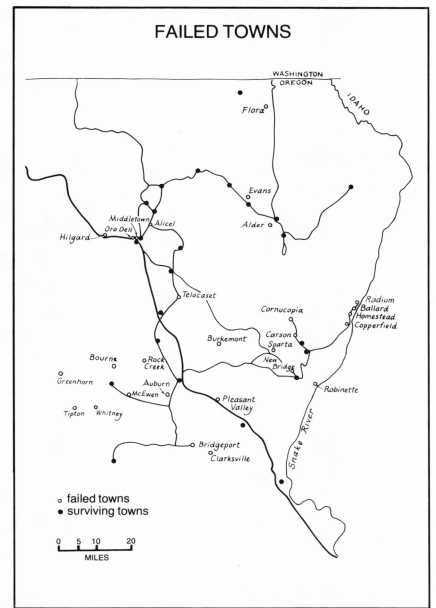

FAILED TOWNS

Fig. 24

WASHINGTON
OREGON

IDAHO

Flora

Evans

Middletown   Alicel
Oro Dell   Alder
Hilgard

Telocaset

Cornucopia   Radium
                              Ballard
                              Homestead
Burkemont   Carson   Copperfield
                    Sparta

Bourne   Rock   New
              Creek   Bridge
Greenhorn
              Auburn   Robinette
              McEwen
                          Pleasant
Tipton Whitney   Valley

                    Bridgeport
                    Clarksville

○ failed towns
● surviving towns

0   5   10   20
MILES

Snake River

63

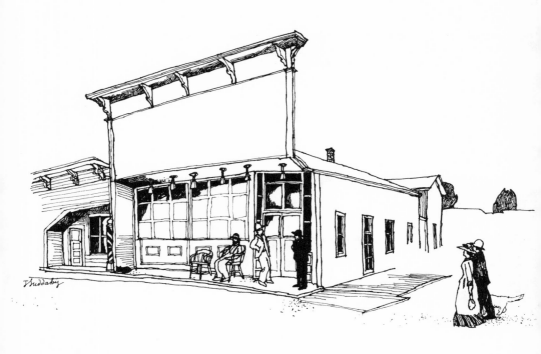

The
Growth of
Towns _____

III

P<small>UBLISHED</small> IN 1902, *An Illustrated History of Union and Wallowa Counties* explained that

> postoffices have been established at other points over the country. With the exception of Flora, none of these places have as yet developed into trade centers of importance. Their future development, however, is almost a certainty. They only await the advent of railroads, the coming of immigrants, the occupancy of the land in small tracts and the consequent need of supply depots, when they will begin to contend with their older neighbors for supremacy as commercial centers of wallowa county (p.512):

When the towns in northeastern Oregon were founded, it seemed reasonable to anticipate their growth, although not all anticipation was as certain as the statement quoted above. With the region populating rapidly, every town seemed likely to thrive. Those that had not immediately grown were expected to do so in the future, for the entire history of frontier settlement spoke of growth. What was not taken into account in 1902 was that settlers often moved on after they realized an areas's limitations. So towns were platted, local speculators platted additions in their own names, merchants opened their shops, and they all waited for business.

Town growth can be measured in many ways. Three means are used here: population, town area and number of businesses. Population is the most familiar measure of growth. However, increased population is not necessarily the earliest manifestation of town growth. As soon as people are convinced that a town has "prospects," they prepare for them. In northeastern Oregon the first symptom of growth was usually an increase in town area as speculators platted additions. Also, hopeful merchants often opened their shops in advance of an adequate supply of local customers, anticipating an expanding rural population as well as increasing numbers of town residents.

Population Growth

The population of a town and the character of its main street are linked. A large number of studies by geographers across the country have found that the larger a town's population, the more business establishments the town contains and the greater the selection of specialized businesses. The studies have even established fairly close relationships between a town's population, the precise types of business present, and the regional importance of the town. Thus, a town's population figures can be used to predict the characteristics of the town's main street. Past population figures help explain the nature of many small town main streets today.*

In general, the larger the town, the wider its influence in the region. While people in smaller towns shop locally for things purchased almost daily, they go farther to larger towns to purchase more expensive and infrequently sought goods and services. Thus the influence of larger towns spreads over a larger area. Serving rural residents and nearby smaller towns, their

---

*The most reliable population figures are those published by the U.S. Census Bureau. However, towns were listed in the census only if they were incorporated. Some towns did not incorporate until 20 or 30 years after founding and so were not separately tabulated in the census until long after they were established. The census of 1910 was the first to include nearly all of the larger towns in the area and after that there is no doubt as to how their populations changed. Before 1910, and for the smaller towns, supplementary sources must be used. One excellent source is the schedules kept by the census takers as they worked their way through the counties. Among other facts, census schedules list the name and occupation of every county resident. This makes it possible to identify the clusters of merchants and tradesmen in the small towns that were not separately reported. Another source is old business directories. The directories must be interpreted with caution however, for their population figures are often inflated by the inclusion of the rural population served by the town's post office. These figures may reflect the population served by the town and be of

66

main street business districts have a population base far greater than that of their own towns' alone. In fact, the size of the population and business district depends on this broader base. By knowing something either about a town's population, its main street characteristics, or its regional importance, a great deal more can be understood about the town.

The edifices seen along main streets today make more sense if the old relationships between population, main street characteristics and regional roles are recognized. Today, some small towns in northeastern Oregon have main streets lined with many large, old buildings that seem out of keeping with the town's present small size and slight regional importance, while the main streets of others that are now larger consist of only a few old structures surrounded by many new business buildings. These apparent main street inconsistencies reflect the age, growth patterns, and past and present roles of the towns (see **table 7**).

In northeastern Oregon the development of a town's main street was influenced by many things. The development of the regional economy was supremely important, for it attracted people to the region and generated wealth. Also significant was competition from nearby towns. Within the town, important influences included the time span during which the town grew, the rate of growth and the size of the town involved. The history

more use than figures for the town's population alone. However, to maintain some consistency with the U.S. Census, the directory figures are corrected here by the subtraction of cattle-, sheep- and horse-raiser statistics. The number thus derived gives an impression of the size of the town. The table of population presented here (**table 7**) has been compiled from several sources: *Oregon Business Directory* (Portland, 1873); *Oregon State Directory* (Portland, 1881); *Oregon, Washington and Idaho Gazetteer and Business Directory, 1891-1892* (Portland, 1891); *Oregon, Washington and Alaska Gazetteer and Business Directory, 1901-02* (Portland, 1901); *Oregon and Washington State Gazetteer and Business Directory, 1913-14* (Seattle, 1913); *Polk's Oregon and Washington State Gazetteer and Business Directory, 1923-24* (Seattle, 1923); *Bradstreet's Book of Commercial Ratings* (New York, 1915, 1926, 1932); U.S. Department of Commerce, Bureau of the Census, *United States Census of Population*, "Number of Inhabitants: Oregon," 1860-1970; Center for Population Research and Census, "Population Estimates of Counties and Incorporated Cities of Oregon" (Portland, 1975).

of main streets shows that when towns grew quickly, they were considered good places in which to invest, and it was during these times that construction occurred; once growth ceased, changes on main street more frequently represented abandonment than construction.

Population trends for the towns still existing in 1970 are shown in figure 25. Nearly all of the towns, like their surrounding districts, show little or no growth after 1920. The years before 1920 constitute the principal period of regional and town population growth in northeastern Oregon and therefore of town and main street construction; the growth patterns that emerged during those years largely determined the nature of main streets.

Three patterns of population growth emerged among the towns that still exist while different patterns are evident in the towns that failed. Most of the surviving towns started out similarly, experiencing rapid growth in their early years. By the end of 10 or 15 years of development, however, their growth rates diverged. Some towns continued to grow rapidly while in others growth slowed or even ceased. It seems to have taken a decade or so for settlers to evaluate the long-term potential of new towns and their districts and the growth patterns after that represented their consensus.

Sustained rapid growth occurred in towns that served an area extending beyond the adjacent rural districts. These had an important regional role and their growth represented the magnitude of their importance. Two, Union and Enterprise, were county seats. Union continued to grow even after it lost its county seat status to La Grande in 1904. Elgin's early rapid growth was boosted by its railhead location serving all of Wallowa County. Wallowa and Joseph both served sizable sections of Wallowa County, their economic base augmented by the large lumber mills that were built after the railroad reached Joseph.

Many towns grew more slowly and less steadily than the rapid-growth towns. These slow-growth towns failed to establish the regional roles of their larger competitors. Although some of them experienced a brief and modest population decline immediately after initial founding, growth was generally maintained

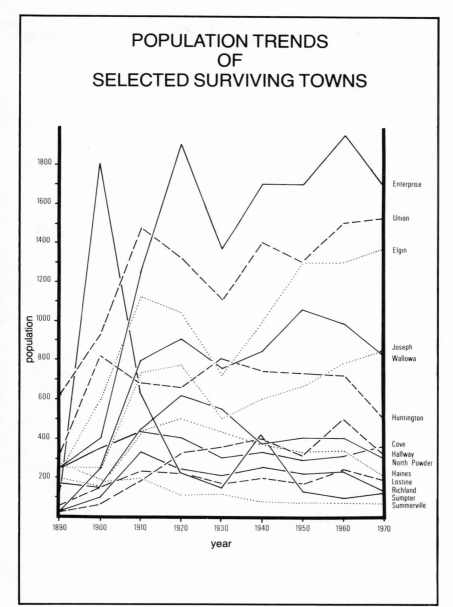

POPULATION TRENDS
OF
SELECTED SURVIVING TOWNS

Fig. 25

population

1800

1600

1400

1200

1000

800

600

400

200

1890   1900   1910   1920   1930   1940   1950   1960   1970

year

Enterprise

Union

Elgin

Joseph
Wallowa

Huntington

Cove
Halfway
North Powder
Haines
Lostine
Richland
Sumpter
Summerville

69

after the 10 or 15 year evaluation period. Since several of these towns were platted after 1900, their growth period was abbreviated due to the general decline in the whole region starting in the 1920s.

North Powder, Haines, Cove, Richland and Halfway are slow-growth towns. North Powder and Haines grew to be the largest of the five. With their railside locations that made them the shipping points for the grain and livestock produced in southern Union and northern Baker counties, they might have developed as rapidly as Joseph and Wallowa.* However, proximity to Union and to the region's two dominant cities, Baker and La Grande, stunted their growth. Cove, Richland and Halfway were purely rural service centers. Cove grew as the cherry and prune orchards around it prospered. Although Richland and Halfway were founded late, amid the flurry of railroad construction and mining excitement in eastern Baker County in the early 1900s, they survived as their rural hinterlands developed.

Eight towns exist today that after the initial founding period experienced no further growth. Despite their failure to grow after their first 10 or 15 years , they have all survived because of their importance to the small section of the county each serves. With only a small resident population, each town clearly is supported by the business it does with the surrounding rural population. Durkee and Summerville, both bypassed by major highways today, continue to function as local service centers. Unity, Imnaha and Troy all lie in distant, isolated parts of their counties, free of competition from nearby towns. Island City, Imbler and Lostine, although near larger towns, are in the middle of productive valleys with relatively large rural populations. In the 1970s several (Island City, Summerville, Imbler and Lostine) showed remarkable growth. This recent growth was based on a new trend: the development of bedroom communities for commuters who work in the larger towns nearby. For the long-time residents, however, custom, convenience and a sense of commu-

---

*North Powder had an additional, unique role: ice from a large pond, harvested throughout the winter, cooled Pacific Fruit Express refrigerator cars for most of the company's rail route across Oregon. When the icehouse burned in the 1930s, North Powder lost an important source of income.

Fig. 26

Ice plant loading platform, North Powder. North Powder ice chilled refrigerator cars all the way from Huntington to Portland. The ice was made during the winter, when a low area outside the plant was flooded with water and allowed to freeze; ice blocks were then sawn and stored in the large ice house. Brought by conveyer belt to the tall platform in front of the ice house, the ice blocks were dropped into rail cars below. (OHS neg. 16881)

nity continue to make these very small towns important local business and social centers.

The towns that failed had different growth patterns from those that have survived. One of two was typical: no growth, or quick growth followed by swift decline. The first pattern, the more common, generally involved hinterland towns platted after 1890. Although some of these towns never attracted any settlers at all, more commonly they did draw a few merchants and a few households. Their populations never rose above 100, however, and as it became apparent that their hinterlands were unable to support them, the towns declined and failed. The second pattern—explosive growth and swift decline—was experienced primarily by mining and logging towns. In some cases these towns exceeded 300 people, but only briefly. Only one town that failed, Flora, began similarly to the towns that have survived. Flora grew more slowly than most, but after 20 years had a busy main street and approximately 175 residents. It seemed certain to follow in the footsteps of Richland and Halfway, both surviving towns. However, the rural population base of Flora, only about half that of Richland and Halfway, subsequently declined, and the town failed.

Between 1970 and 1980, population increased in nearly all of the region's towns, with Union County recording the greatest growth, especially for the towns closest to La Grande. This growth, which reflects a national trend of small-town growth as young people elect to remain in their native region and urban refugees seek simpler, more pleasant places to live, has had an impact on northeastern Oregon's main streets, resulting in changes that will be discussed in Chapter 6.

Growth in Area

Once a town was platted and growth commenced, it expanded in area as well as in population. Local speculators assessed the boom-to-be and then platted their land as additions to the town, often before settlers arrived to occupy these areas. Frequently, too few people arrived to fill the additions, resulting in a situation where residences extended to a town's boundaries but with low densities. In some cases, additions were vacated because growth halted before any lots were sold. Very few additions were platted after 1910.

The platting of, and additions to, the towns of northeastern Oregon are indicated in table 8. Three patterns emerge. The earlier towns expanded gradually. Their populations were small, and each addition contained sufficient land to accommodate new residents. The middle group of towns, which was founded in the middle and late 1880s, experienced rapid areal expansion 10 or 20 years later. In this group, the rapid speculative expansion of Sumpter accompanied the mining boom, and the relatively late growth of Enterprise and Wallowa demonstrates once more that the development of Wallowa County lagged somewhat behind that of Baker and Union counties. The third pattern was that of no growth. Only a few towns platted after 1895 grew enough to reasonably merit additions. Richland had four small additions and Halfway seven; Flora's lone addition was later vacated and is now a pasture.

Platted additions to growing towns generally kept pace with population increases so that density remained relatively constant. In fact, up to 1910 the areas of some towns grew much faster than their populations. After 1910, there were some variations, however. Union's area has not changed significantly since 1892, but its population has tripled. Elgin's area has been virtually the same since 1897, but its population tripled between 1900 and 1980. The areal expansion of Wallowa County's towns more closely paralleled population growth. Enterprise's flurry of additions between 1915 and 1920 was accompanied by a corresponding population increase. Its population peaked in 1920 at a level not reached again until 1980, so its residential districts' densities in 1980 about equaled what they were in the early 1900s. (An examination of these residential districts is interesting, for this indicates what kind of neighborhoods were considered most desirable between 1910 and 1920.)

Much of the impression of a town's size comes from the area it covers. With their numerous platted additions, many of these small towns seem larger than their populations would necessitate. In most towns, population growth halted for almost 40 years (until the decade of the 1970s) and only Enterprise and Elgin have developed anything resembling a suburban fringe.* In the other towns, new home construction has taken place within the platted additions; this has kept the edges of these towns distinct. However, within town boundaries, the residential districts still present a pastoral appearance. As additions were platted, homeowners often purchased several adjacent lots, creating an open residential pattern that provided unrestricted views to the edges of town. The sight of large woodpiles, vegetable gardens and barns is still common in these towns, as are the sounds of farm animals kept as 4-H projects. The open character of

---

*In the last ten years, additions have been made to Island City, Imbler and Union. This reflects La Grande's growth; these towns, particularly Island City, have developed as bedroom communities.

Fig. 27

Residential neighborhood, Wallowa, about 1920. Main street runs across the center of the photograph in front of the two-story high school—downtown lies one block to the right, off the photograph. The houses and barns in the foreground stand in an addition platted in 1906. The rural character of northeastern Oregon towns shows up even today in the wide spaces between houses and the numerous barns, barbed wire fences, and unpaved residential streets. (OHS neg. 18867)

residential districts contrasts with the density of main street. The main streets of northeastern Oregon stand out as distinct units, sharply defined in all directions, and surrounded in turn by towns that are both well defined and, in many ways, continuations of the countryside.

Growth in Business Activities

An increase in the number and prosperity of a town's businesses is popularly accepted as an indication of growth. The relationship between population and the size and structure of a business community is complex, however. Doubling a population

Fig. 28

Main street, Elgin, about 1915. Elgin, a pioneer town, was founded in 1886 along the road from La Grande to Wallowa County. Located along this main route (soon paralleled by a rail line), Elgin grew quickly and soon surpassed Summerville as the largest town in northern Union County. As a social and commercial center, its main street developed rapidly. The gradually changing structure of Elgin's business community between 1900 and 1910, tallied along with those of Enterprise, Joseph and Union, is indicated in table 9. This photograph illustrates the social role. Chatting pedestrians are dispersing probably after viewing a parade (the band is still playing in the distance). The lingering crowd and the signs on the buildings for ice cream, a restaurant and a movie matinee, confirm that main street was a place for pleasurable gatherings and recreation as well as commerce. (OHS neg. 15528)

will not result in a doubling of the number of business establishments. This is because, for their survival, certain businesses require a greater population base than others. As the towns of northeastern Oregon developed, the number and variety of business that opened exceeded the number that could be supported by the population. Times must have been difficult for the early merchants, who faced rapid changes in transportation routes and competition from newly founded towns nearby.

The changing character of the main street business community can be understood by examining the businesses along four northeastern Oregon main streets. The businesses lining the main streets of Elgin, Enterprise, Joseph and Union were tallied for 1900 and 1910 (**table 9**).* During this time, the total population of these towns increased 61 percent, but the number of businesses increased only 27 percent. The total population of the census divisions holding the towns increased 33 percent, suggesting that the business community's growth corresponded more closely to the growth of the district surrounding the town than to that of the town itself. However, a closer look at the composition of the business community indicates that its internal structure altered as it grew. Those services catering to townfolk became more numerous, while those relating to the needs of the general populace, including both rural and town residents, remained relatively constant.

Certain business activities showed little or no increase downtown. Trade in general stores diminished slightly with the appearance of more specialized stores, but the total number of businesses selling the same goods remained virtually the same. The first seven activities listed under "Commercial Activities" in table 9 totaled 26 in 1900 and 25 in 1910. The number of hardware stores, tin shops and drugstores increased slightly. The greatest increases, however, occurred in businesses related to town construction and furnishing (carpentry, furniture, paints, oils and wallpaper) and those associated with the increasing

---

*The tally was based on maps published by the Sanborn Map Company. Several of the items listed in the tally do not appear in any of the towns in either period. They were included in the tally because they occurred on main streets of other towns of the time, and their absence is indicative of the nature of the towns considered. The towns were selected because of their comparable Sanborn coverage and roughly equivalent size. Enterprise and Joseph, only six miles apart, can be considered a single, complementary unit. The towns are consolidated in the table in order to present larger patterns than individual town statistics would.

76

Fig. 29

Business district, Joseph. This photograph of Wallowa County's south-ernmost town, founded in 1883, shows the spacious lots and scattered placement of business establishments in a pioneer town. Joseph was founded to serve Wallowa County's rural population, and, along with three other Wallowa Valley towns, provided major services for the districts to the north and east. In 1900, 237 people resided in Joseph; the railroad reached the town in 1908 and by the end of the decade its population had more than tripled. (OHS neg. 16033)

wealth of town residents (banks and jewelers). There were more bakeries in 1910, and the reduction in notions shops was more than compensated for by the number of their more appealing successor, the confectionery—which usually combined the sale of notions and candy with a soda fountain.

Several conclusions may be drawn from this tally about the growth and prosperity of the business districts in northeastern Oregon's small towns. When a town was founded, it attracted a group of merchants who opened shops that fulfilled the basic needs of the entire region: general stores, butcher shops and blacksmiths. The population in the towns and surrounding districts could not have comfortably supported even these at first; however, as growth occurred, the existing stores absorbed the increasing business, and presumably prospered. But the population increase also attracted other businesses, which filled out main street. These later arrivals, more specialized, were oriented toward the townspeople. But the economic health of the town continued to depend on support from residents of the surrounding area. (Only when a town developed a form of industry, such as lumber, did it achieve some independence from its rural hinterland.)

In the 1880s and '90s, news of the platting or founding of a town would have been received with interest by merchants seeking new opportunities. They knew that the earliest established businessmen had the advantage, with a chance to build up their capital, stock and clientele. Hence the rush into these new towns and the main street development. All too often, however, once a town was started, not much happened. Population stabilized after the initial period of settlement. Business did not increase sufficiently to support all of the shops. Thus, despite the enthusiasm surrounding the founding of small towns and early development of their main streets, subsequent main street prosperity was not assured. Some merchants were forced to seek new towns, and the process began again elsewhere.

Summary

The small towns of northeastern Oregon were founded with high hopes. Their founders, envisioning important futures for these towns, profited from the sale of lots. Small merchants arrived early on, anxious to establish themselves before others did in order to increase their chances of success. To prepare for the anticipated influx of settlers, additions were platted, increasing a town's area, sometimes doubling or even quadrupling it. The only missing ingredient, to complete these plans, was an adequate population in the towns and surrounding countrysides. In some cases, the visions materialized: people arrived, settled both in the towns and outlying areas, and, as a result, the towns grew. More often, however, the surrounding region grew too slowly to support substantial town growth. In these cases, the towns did not grow much beyond the size they reached after their original burst of development. The towns lingered on, diminishing gradually. Those that still exist retain their local importance, however, and thus have not failed altogether.

The
Development of
Main Street

IV

EVERY SMALL TOWN in northeastern Oregon has a main street whose physical structure and associated activities have undergone a number of changes. These changes follow identifiable patterns. A detailed examination of change along main streets clarifies these patterns and the sequence of their development. It leads to an understanding of how main streets reached their present state and of their significance today. This chapter addresses the physical development of main street; the following chapter discusses the street's economic and social functions.

Main street was an integral part of the concept of towns in northeastern Oregon, and generally was designated by the town platters. As merchants and speculators arrived, the main street lots were quickly sold and resold, and buildings gradually filled in these sites. If the main street prospered, early construction was gradually replaced by newer buildings. The styles and materials of main street buildings accurately indicate the period (or periods) of main street construction.

The changes in a main street's physical structure correspond to the intensity of land use along it. As a town grew, the structures along its main street became both larger and more tightly packed, eventually eliminating open space frontage. Building density peaked around 1920. Since building density can be correlated with town size, it is possible today, by looking at the old buildings along a main street, to identify the size and regional role of the town 60 years ago and to reconstruct its main street.

The Selection of Main Street

Most northeastern Oregon towns were platted near an existing road, which then was often rerouted locally to coincide with one of the town's new streets; generally this road became the main street. In different towns its position varied. Some main streets passed along the edge of the town, while others were more centrally located.

Plats of northeastern Oregon towns usually employed a grid system oriented north, south, east and west. Only the mining and railroad towns adjusted their orientation according to factors such as terrain or railroad routes. The region's early roads had been laid down before the township and range system standardized road directions. Thus, when a town was platted, the route had to be modified locally to conform to the town's grid. The platter usually decided that the rerouted road would become the town's main street and travel its length, and then he determined its placement in his town. In general, the towns founded earliest and latest had main streets that passed along their margins; the main streets of towns platted in the 1880s ran through the center of town. The earlier and later towns, platted small, initially depended on road traffic for support. Only a few of these towns later platted additions across the road from the original town, enclosing and transforming it into a centrally located main street. The towns of the 1880s, and some of the later ones, were platted on a grander scale and the local main road was realigned to proceed formally through their centers.

Main street was labeled on most of the town plats. Of 35 town plats examined, 26 identified it by name; on 21 of the 26 the street was called "Main Street," and on 14 others it was called "Front Street" (these latter stood beside the road or fronted on railyards). In North Powder, the main street was designated "Center Street."

On plats, main streets were usually distinguishable only by name; they generally matched the others in width, measuring from 60 to 100 feet. The plat of Enterprise is the only one in which lot size indicates the expected location of the downtown business district; the standard town lot width is 60 feet, but the width of lots lining the main street and the courthouse square only 30 feet.

In only a few cases did main street develop along a different street from the one planned. Cove was platted without reference to the through road that served it, and the platted main street was several blocks from the one that eventually developed along the through road. North Powder's Center Street, identifiable on the plat as the main street by both name and greater width, became a residential street, superseded by E Street because of the latter's proximity to the railroad depot. In Elgin, the main street platted in 1885 developed as such but two fires and the 1891 arrival of the railroad resulted in development along a street in Hindman's Addition, a subsequently platted area between the original town and the railroad depot. Enterprise's main street grew up in its initially assigned location; however, the business-width lots around two sides of the courthouse square were only lightly built up, since the business district actually developed along the route of the highway, which ran along only part of the officially designated main street.

Main street selection was a fundamental part of town planning in northeastern Oregon; without a main street, a place would not have been considered a town. The frequency of its identification on plats indicates that planners recognized its important role and expected it to be the center of trade for a wide area. Usually, the main street was deliberately platted to coincide with the road that connected the town with the surrounding district and the region beyond.

The Sale of Main Street

Main street lots sold surprisingly quickly once a town was platted. Despite sparse population in the immediate area, lots along main street went rapidly and the business district was soon delineated. Frequently, the original purchasers quickly resold these lots, at a profit. Clearly, speculation played a significant part in the early development of main streets.

Union and Summerville exemplify towns in which speculation in main street lots occurred. Both were platted beside roads by men with small businesses already established along them. Union was strategically situated beside one of the traces of the Oregon Trail, and Summerville stood along the Ruckles Road, which connected northeastern Oregon with Walla Walla (at the

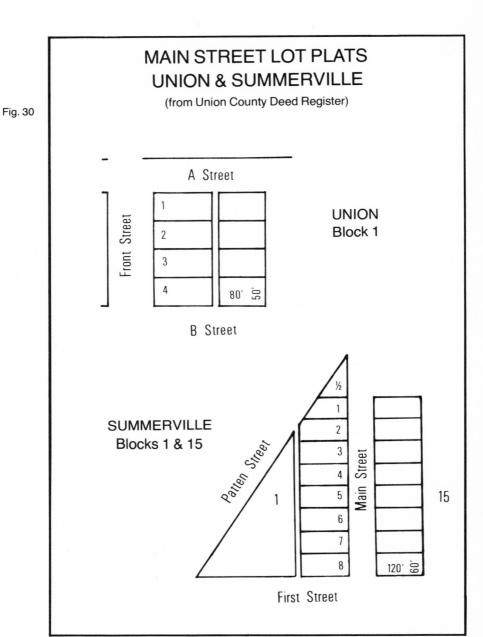

MAIN STREET LOT PLATS
UNION & SUMMERVILLE
(from Union County Deed Register)

Fig. 30

A Street

Front Street

1
2
3
4

80' 50'

UNION
Block 1

B Street

SUMMERVILLE
Blocks 1 & 15

Patten Street

1

½
1
2
3
4
5
6
7
8

Main Street

15

120' 60'

First Street

time an important supply center for much of eastern Oregon). Each town was supported by passing traffic and local trade.

Union's plat was filed November 11, 1864, by John Chapman, and the first lots were sold within the month. Several lots were sold for only $1.00, implying that they were already held by their purchaser, and Chapman was only technically transferring title (it is expectable that a pioneer town would have several merchants already established by the time of legal platting). An examination of Block 1 in Union (**fig. 30**) indicates that all four lots facing Front Street (as Union's main street had been named), the prime commercial lots, were sold within six months of platting. Fifty feet wide, they were subject to subdivision from the outset. Lot 3 was split into two 25-foot parcels and then sold to two separate parties on December 8, 1864.[17]

As Union prospered in the 1860s, the lots along its main street changed hands frequently. Of course, Union's main street business district soon extended beyond the four lots in Block 1. Within that block, however, the four lots (and fractions thereof) changed hands 11 times by 1870. The increased value of the lots at resale indicates that they were probably built on in the interval. Chapman's standard price for an undeveloped lot was $50. Main street lots in Block 1 were sold by later owners in the 1860s for prices up to $500 and $900. Clearly, main street property values escalated quickly in a thriving pioneer town.

Summerville's plat (**fig. 30**) was filed almost 10 years after Union's on September 20, 1873, by William H. Patten, who located the town at the site of Patten's freight station on the Ruckles Road. Political maneuverings had temporarily diverted the main stage route across the Blues from the Oregon Trail to this road. This put Union on the main stage line and La Grande on a branch line, enabling Union to become the county seat by election in 1874. The route shift also temporarily increased the accessibility of the northern Grande Ronde Valley, and made Summerville an attractive townsite along a major road.

Despite the seemingly advantageous town location, the lots in Summerville sold more slowly than those in Union. The business district developed in the lots of blocks 1, 2 and 15 facing the Ruckles Road (which through town was its main street). Merchants purchased the lots along blocks 1 and 15; Block 2 became

Fig. 31

Guests gather for an evening social hour on the front porch of "Grandma McRae's House," a log hotel at Meacham in Umatilla County. Built in a southern tradition with finely worked logs, this large hotel stood along the Oregon Trail at the crest of the Blue Mountains. (Courtesy of the Walter M. Pierce Library, Eastern Oregon State College)

the site of a hotel and livery stable. The lots of blocks 1 and 15 faced one another across main street and were purchased at about the same time, and the street developed along both sides simultaneously. While all of Union's main street lots had been sold almost as soon as they were platted, it took Patten nine years to sell Summerville's sixteen lots in blocks 1 and 15. Sales were slow in Summerville from the first. Three lots were sold in November, 1873, one in March, 1874, and another four in the fall of 1874. By the end of that year, only eight of the available sixteen lots had been purchased. These eight lots were not contiguous; widely spaced, they spanned the main street business district. To their south, Block 2 was also selling slowly. Favored lots changed hands several times before Patten made some of the initial sales on others. In Block 1, for example, Lot 1 changed hands four times between its initial purchase in November, 1873 and March, 1877, and its price rose from Patten's original $50 to $350. Altogether, the eight lots of Block 1 changed hands twenty-one times by the time Patten sold the last of them in 1882.[18]

Despite their location along the same road, Union and Summerville were different towns in different situations. Union was able to compete for and win the county seat. It supplied the mining districts to the south and east. And its lots sold and developed quickly. Summerville's significance rested solely as its role as a travelers' stop and supplier for a lightly settled agricultural district. Its lots sold more slowly than Union's, but in both towns the lots' resale value increased as buildings were added. In general, lots in both towns changed hands rapidly and frequently as speculators and merchants stayed only briefly. The turnover rate was high. In Summerville, only four of the twenty-one persons who bought lots from 1873 to 1885 still owned main street land in 1902. The early speculators left Summerville in the mid-1880s because the Ruckles Road over the Blues washed out in 1884 and Elgin was platted in 1886. Elgin soon became the favored town and target of speculation.

Main Street Buildings

Buildings enter into this study principally as indicators of the main street development process. For this purpose, only the basic facts about them—their relative dimensions, basic style and construction materials—are necessary; a careful analysis of the style and architecture has not been included.*

The smaller towns of the region lacked the financial resources

---

*Architecturally, the most interesting buildings in northeastern Oregon are found in two cities not covered by this study: Baker and La Grande. Baker, which developed as the "capital" of eastern Oregon, contains many fine public buildings built of stone in a Richardsonian style as well as a twin-spired, stone cathedral and several fine buildings along its main street. La Grande, which developed in the shadow of Baker, had buildings that lacked the grandeur of those in Baker, but the city's turn-of-the-century main street was a monument of Victoriana, with cast-iron statuary in its central intersection and buildings laden with splendid cornices and topped by cupolas. (Today, several of the cornices remain but the statues and cupolas are gone.)

Fig. 32

On the road between Wallowa County and Lewiston, Idaho, the Paradise
Hotel provided typical accommodations for frontier travelers. (Courtesy
of the Walter M. Pierce Library, Eastern Oregon State College)

to build elaborate buildings. In the smaller towns, attention to
style and decoration was devoted chiefly to the lodge halls that
frequently appeared along their main streets. Otherwise, buildings were similar in character, repeating basic architectural patterns seen widely throughout the West. What makes these buildings interesting is the sequence of their appearance in a town,
information useful in interpreting main street evolution.

Log Construction

Northeastern Oregon's first structures presumably were log
buildings. Log construction, typical of pioneer settlement, is correlated with a stage of settlement rather than with a particular
time period. For example, in Wallowa County's northern end,
which at the time was only recently settled, houses, barns, school
houses and hotels were still being built of logs in 1910 while large

The Hafer ranch house, a carefully constructed log structure occupied at this time by the family posed in front of it, was built in a section of northern Wallowa County that since has been largely abandoned. Notice the tangle of hop vines that have been pulled down beneath the windows. This house was entirely contemporary in style. It was built of logs because sawn lumber was unavailable. (Courtesy of the Walter M. Pierce Library, Eastern Oregon State College)

brick and stone buildings were going up in Enterprise, the county seat.

Some of the log structures were well finished while others were only roughly worked. Old photographs of two hotels indicate the range of craftsmanship, which depended on the builder's resources and skills. Figure 31 shows "Grandma McRae's House," a large log hotel on the Oregon Trail at Meacham, the summit of the Blue Mountains, just outside the Union County line. Designed in a southern style, it contains a central hall and end chimneys. The hotel is constructed of finished hewn logs joined by the durable half dove-tail notch, a precise, time-consuming process. Log structures of this fine workmanship were often second-generation buildings, replacing simpler structures that had been hastily erected under more primitive conditions.

The photograph of the Paradise Hotel (**fig. 32**) was taken in about 1910. This hotel, built along the road to Lewiston, Idaho at Paradise, Wallowa County, differs from the hotel at Meacham in a number of ways. Small and humble, it is reminiscent in form, although not in finish, of a small Pennsylvania Dutch central-chimney house. It is built of partially trimmed logs, fastened at the corners by what appear to be simple saddle notches, which could be hastily cut, but rotted quickly. Not all log structures in northern Wallowa County were so plainly fashioned. The Hafer Ranch House (**fig. 33**) stood alongside Cabin Creek, in the Garden of Eden section southwest of Troy. With its height, fashionable proportions and bay window, it might have stood in town instead of on the frontier, had it been built of sawn lumber rather than home-hewn logs.

Today, a number of log buildings (mainly barns and cribs) still stand in northeastern Oregon, but most are in poor repair. Some log houses are still in use but exterior siding and interior paneling complicate identification and examination of their original construction.

Wood-Frame Construction

A town's earliest commercial buildings generally were built of sawn lumber, for a sawmill was one of the first industries established in the vicinity of a new town. As a town grew, it attracted carpenters, and perhaps stonemasons and bricklayers, all of whom contributed their skills to the town's construction. Buildings of wood remained more common than those of stone or brick, however, for the material and the skills to work it were the most universal. Nevertheless, a number of stone and brick structures went up in the larger towns.

The earliest main street buildings were usually small and domestic in character. In effect, they were houses converted to shops. The early main street had only a few buildings along it, casually placed on their lots. As space along the street became more valuable, the buildings were more carefully situated in re-

Fig. 34

The gable-ended building, a standard structure that appeared along many main streets, was adapted for a variety of purposes, ranging from lodge halls to hotels, general stores to saloons. This Lostine building housed the Wallowa County Real Estate Co.; the second floor was used as the school house. In 1902 the building was moved and became Crows Store. (OHS neg. 26814)

lationship to the lot margins and a standard commercial building emerged: an oblong structure placed gable-end to the street. Eventually, several buildings fronting on main street would rise on a single lot, and widths and depths became standardized. The maximum depth of a frame structure was about three times its street width. Even when a building was freestanding, its width to depth proportion ranged from 1:2 to 1:3. Figure 34 displays one of these typical two-story frame buildings (this one, erected in Lostine, was moved in 1902 and, although much modified, is still in use).

False fronts often finished the street-facing gable ends of main street buildings, adding height and a sense of continuity and substance to the street. Figure 35 shows a typical row of false-front buildings in Richland (most of them are still in use).

Fig. 35

False fronts in Richland finish off main street's otherwise standard gable-end buildings. The fronts added height and presence to each structure and, by filling out the skyline, added substance to the street's appearance. (OHS neg. 17742)

The only frame buildings not constructed gable end to the street were hotels, which were consistently designed with their roof ridge paralleling the street. This may have served to enhance their domestic image. In any case, it increased their main street frontage and hence their visibility, particularly desirable because the first floor of hotels usually contained a number of small shops or offices; greater frontage permitted more offices to face on the street.

Stone and Brick Construction

Two types of stone were used in northeastern Oregon building construction, both of local origin: granite and consolidated volcanic ash (the ash was the more common). The granite came from a quarry near Haines. This dark, fine-grained stone, heavy and difficult to work, was incorporated principally as trim on

Fig. 36

The Wallowa County Courthouse, with a side fronting on the town's main street, still stands at 101 S. River Street in Enterprise. It was made to look properly substantial with its stone construction, accented by the use of wood trim and fine detailing. (OHS neg. 15342)

brick buildings. (A granite building of fine workmanship still stands, however, on the main street of Haines.)

Buildings of consolidated volcanic ash are more common in the region. This light gray ash has many desirable characteristics. Almost as lightweight as wood, the stone, when wet, is soft enought to cut with a saw. Nails can even be driven into it. This building material did present some problems, however. Its popular use for chimney construction, prior to the discovery that it gradually burned away, accounts for the origin of many destructive house fires.[19]

Buildings constructed of ash were not finely finished despite the ease with which the stone could be worked; the treatment was heavy, with massive chunks of the material. The front usually displayed roughly dressed stone while the sides were laid with rubble courses. Rarely was pattern introduced to the facade through decoration or variety in the courses or arches. The Lostine School is a colorful exception with its use of contrasting red ash for a string course, corner quoins and crossing diagonals. The Wallowa County Courthouse (**fig. 36**) presents perhaps the region's most harmonious blend of stone with a high Victorian style; its stone construction, emphasizing the building's mass, is accented by wood trim in the deep, pedimented gables, fan lights and tower.

Brick (see **fig. 37**) was used more frequently and with more variety of design than stone in northeastern Oregon. Small local brickyards produced soft, easily weathered brick, occasionally employed in house construction but more commonly in commercial buildings. Whereas the texture of stone provided surface interest, the smooth brick relied on pattern to impart interest. The sophistication with which brick construction was handled varied from town to town; unfortunately, information concerning the region's bricklayers is sparse.

The stylistic shifts in brick buildings are more pronounced than in the wood or stone buildings. In northeastern Oregon, the design of wooden commercial buildings stemmed from that of domestic structures. Changes in their design resulted largely from the adoption of certain stylistic elements initially displayed by the Victorian house. Northeastern Oregon's brick buildings, however, had a separate, distinct tradition. They were simply the country cousins of their high-style city counterparts, and their facades presented a vernacular interpretation of the fashionable brick city building.

The brick buildings built in northeastern Oregon before 1900 incorporated various Italianate elements into their facades and ornamentation, typically featuring arched windows and bracketed cornices. The more elaborate buildings possessed cast-iron cornices. Union provides the best examples from this period. Between 1900 and about 1915, the brickwork became more elaborate while the Italianate elements disappeared. Decorative detail was supplied by variations in courses, surface textures and ash or granite trim. Different towns had different types of decoration, depending on the local bricklayers' talents, and hotels were typically the outlet for the bricklayers' creativity. The Hotel McCrae, built in 1911 in Wallowa (but destroyed by fire in the 1920s), demonstrated a most enthusiastic use of brick with multi-

Fig. 37

As a rule the first brick establishments built along main street were either banks or hotels: this one in Union housed the First National Bank, the Pacific Express Co., an insurance office and the post office. More expensive than wooden structures, brick buildings came to symbolize town wealth, progress and prosperity—published descriptions of towns often included the number of brick buildings that stood along main street. Their construction widely advertised, newly completed brick buildings often were photographed with the proud owners, builders and admiring passersby posed in front. (OHS neg. 54263)

ple arches, chimneys, and a giant corbelled parapet (see **fig. 38**). Joseph also contains a number of brick buildings from this period but the brick buildings of Elgin are probably the era's most sophisticated, with a classical touch in their design and decoration (see **fig. 39**). After 1915, the brick buildings became plainer, only slightly decorated with string courses and recessed panels. Most of the brick buildings of North Powder and Haines originated during this later period.

The earliest buildings on a main street, typically of wood-frame construction, closely resembled houses. Their numbers were soon augmented by commercial buildings placed gable end

Fig. 38

96

Fig. 39

For just over a decade, the Hotel McCrae (fig. 38, facing) was the "leading" hotel in Wallowa, Oregon. Built in 1911, it had the most elaborate
brickwork in town. The oddly syncopated window spacing and sizes on
the first and second floors was typical of small hotel structures, which
were designed to incorporate rented office space on the ground floor
(the left three arches were part of the hotel and the right two were associated with the office). (OHS neg. 48538)

The Sommer Hotel annex in Elgin (second floor shown above) displays
proportions typical of the brick buildings built before 1915. Its ash ac-
cents (as window sills and keystones), with a finish typical of around 1910,
are incorporated into an otherwise classically formal facade. Later brick
buildings were usually lower and plainer, recessed panels their only decoration. (B. R. Bailey)

to the street, a popular architectural solution from the 1870s into
the 1890s. False-front buildings appeared about 10 years later
and were built as late as 1915. Brick buildings, introduced in the
1880s, were built as long as main street construction continued—in some towns into the 1920s. This long time span wit-
nessed some stylistic shifts. Stone buildings, however, erected
between about 1900 and 1915, showed little variation in style.

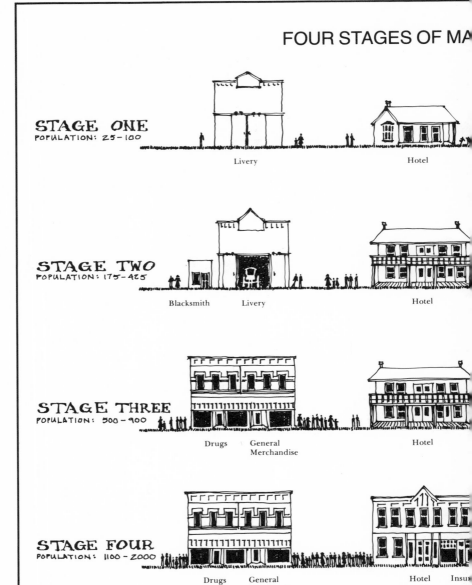

FOUR STAGES OF MA[...]

Fig. 40

STAGE ONE
POPULATION: 25-100

Livery   Hotel

STAGE TWO
POPULATION: 175-425

Blacksmith   Livery   Hotel

STAGE THREE
POPULATION: 500-900

Drugs   General   Hotel
        Merchandise

STAGE FOUR
POPULATION: 1100-2000

Drugs   General   Hotel   Insu[...]
        Merchandise

98

Saloon General Merchandise General Merchandise

Drugs Meat Saloon Barber General Merchandise

oon Billiards General Merchandise Variety Hardware General Merchandise Bank

Variety Groceries Barber and Cigars Jeweler Furniture General Merchandise Bank

As main streets developed, they passed through several construction phases. Thus, the buildings along them provide valuable clues about their evolution. Changes in building materials and style help identify the age of the street, the period during which it was built, and how far along the evolutionary sequence it went.

Physical Development of Main Streets

In their physical evolution, main streets passed through several stages. These corresponded to the town's growth, involving the progression from a relatively open building pattern to a denser one. Four stages of development can be identified in the small towns examined in northeastern Oregon (see **fig. 40**). These stages are not differentiated by any single feature; rather, each represents a different composite of characteristics that developed over the years. As the streets were built and rebuilt, some characteristics from earlier stages lingered while others, more typical of later stages, emerged. Wallowa's 1926 main street, shown in figure 41, exhibited such a composite. Nevertheless, a definite sequence of development changed main streets from a pioneer row of widely spaced, gable-end and false-front frame structures to a solid row of two-story brick business buildings.

Throughout a main street's history, one element remained fairly constant: the portion of the street included in the business district. It was usually two blocks. This two-block length appeared even along the earliest streets. As a business district developed, its length remained the same but the gaps between the buildings were filled with increasing numbers of wider, deeper, taller, buildings. Only in the largest towns did the main street business district ever expand to three or more blocks.*

---

*Beyond the business district on the main streets, there was frequently a zone containing public and institutional buildings such as schools and churches. This area underwent fewer physical changes than the business district, and therefore reveals little about main street evolution.

Fig. 41

Main street, Wallowa, about 1926. A main street is a composite of building styles, identification of which helps to determine the years during
which the street was built. Visible here are a gable-end building (the first
building on the right side), many false fronts, two stone buildings and
two of brick (the two-story Hotel McCrae, in the left foreground, and a
later panel style). The gable-end is probably pre–1900 while the panel
style brick was built in the 1920s. (OHS neg. 18708)

The history of main street involves increasingly intense land
use; therefore the four stages of development relate to building
density and height.

In stage 1 main streets, the business district appeared as an
area of single-story, widely spaced buildings. Of gable-end and
false-front frame construction, they often rose on alternate lots.
When it reached stage 2, the district contained a mixture of sin-
gle- and double-story buildings, less widely spaced. Although a
few gaps still existed, most lots were filled. Some were even subdivided with two buildings on them. A few of the structures were
brick. Stage 3 business districts consisted of mixed single- and
double-story structures, in close proximity to one another.
These buildings, some of them brick and stone, covered a lot's

entire frontage but not the full depth. By stage 4, the area was filled with two-story, tightly packed buildings, most of which were brick or stone and covered a lot's entire width and depth.

Towns that reached the fourth stage progressed through each of the preceding stages. Sometimes features of all four stages appeared simultaneously.

Main street construction continued as long as a town continued to grow, and in some cases even longer. Figure 42 ranks the region's towns by their maximum population and indicates the stage each main street reached.* The appearance of these towns' main streets today correlates with their maximum population in the past. Representatives of each of the four stages still exist in northeastern Oregon (the first stage, however, is preserved only in ghost towns.)

Stage 1 Main Streets of Northeastern Oregon

As has been established, the main street of a new town was often the first developed area. Towns were founded as trading centers and merchants usually built the first buildings. In new towns, the standard business district stretched about two blocks along main street; merchants bought property within that area, selecting non-adjacent lots and creating a main street with many gaps along its length. Their buildings were usually of frame construction with the gable end to the street. Some had false fronts.

Deeds and old photographs provide records of main streets in this early stage. Figure 43, derived from the Union County deed register, indicates the placement of Summerville's first main street buildings. It is based on lot prices at the time of sale. From the records, it is clear that in the 1870s, in the first years of the

---

*The groupings indicated on this diagram are based on common main street characteristics, and in most cases seem consistent with differences in the towns' populations. The only break that might seem arbitrary with respect to population levels occurs between stages 2 and 3. Because Haines and North Powder have main streets more similar to Joseph and Huntington than to Cove and Halfway, they have been included with the former.

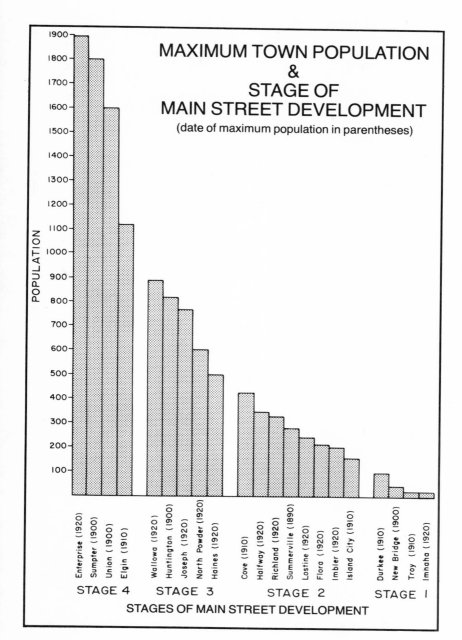

MAXIMUM TOWN POPULATION
&
STAGE OF
MAIN STREET DEVELOPMENT
(date of maximum population in parentheses)

Fig. 42

POPULATION

1900
1800
1700
1600
1500
1400
1300
1200
1100
1000
900
800
700
600
500
400
300
200
100

Enterprise (1920)
Sumpter (1900)
Union (1900)
Elgin (1910)

Wallowa (1920)
Huntington (1900)
Joseph (1920)
North Powder (1920)
Haines (1920)

Cove (1910)
Halfway (1920)
Richland (1920)
Summerville (1890)
Lostine (1920)
Flora (1920)
Imbler (1920)
Island City (1910)

Durkee (1910)
New Bridge (1900)
Troy (1910)
Imnaha (1920)

STAGE 4   STAGE 3   STAGE 2   STAGE 1

STAGES OF MAIN STREET DEVELOPMENT

103

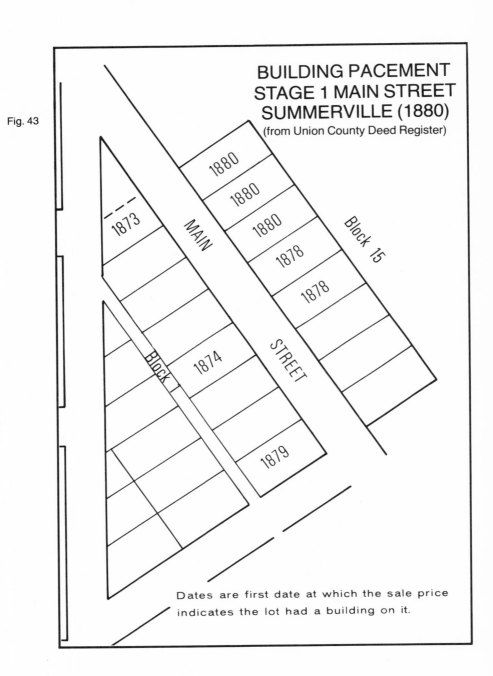

Fig. 43

**BUILDING PACEMENT
STAGE 1 MAIN STREET
SUMMERVILLE (1880)**
(from Union County Deed Register)

Dates are first date at which the sale price
indicates the lot had a building on it.

104

town's existence, the buildings were widely separated. In the 1880s, buildings were built in the intervening spaces.*

A photograph of Elgin, taken shortly after the town was platted in 1885 (**fig. 44**), shows the distribution of buildings along a pioneer main street. It also indicates that this central street was the first part of the town to develop. The main street, in the center of the photograph, runs east-west. It is lined by widely spaced business buildings and livery stables with open fields between and behind them. Fences behind the buildings marked lot boundaries and the northern edge of the platted town. A few houses and a church stand to the south of the main street. The fences beyond them designated the southern margin of the platted town. This is Elgin's original main street (later displaced by one running north-south in the empty land to the right of the street that appears in this photograph).

The pioneer town was a small settlement consisting of a main street with a few wooden frame buildings spread along it, accompanied by a few houses off to the side. The towns that survived soon passed this stage as they grew and their main streets filled in with more buildings.

Stage 2 Main Streets

A number of northeastern Oregon's towns still possess stage 2 main streets, lined with one- and two-story wood-frame buildings among which a few stone or brick buildings of the same height are interspersed. Although buildings stand on nearly all of the lots, there is still open space between them, even where lots have been divided and contain two structures. The main streets are busy despite the towns' small populations, which peaked at from 200 to 450 people sometime between 1890 and 1920. With the exception of Imbler, which is sited on a spur line, these towns

---

*It is assumed that major improvements were added to a lot when its price rose substantially between two sales. The turnover rate was rapid between 1873 and 1883, making it possible to identify the time of initial building construction within a year or two. The price for Summerville lots rose from $50 to $300-$500. Unimproved lots continued to sell at $50, indicating that the increase in price was not due to profiteering on the empty lots.

105

Fig. 44

Stage 1 main street, Elgin, about 1887, looking west up main street. In a pioneer town, main street was the first area to be developed, and in Elgin it was lined by general stores, a livery stable, and a hotel; a church and a few houses completed the town. A sawmill in the vicinity of Elgin (at present the site of a Boise-Cascade plant) provided much of the lumber with which the town's early buildings were constructed. (Courtesy Ethel Chandler, Elgin)

are distant from industry and railroads and their economies have been based on the surrounding districts. Founded for a variety of reasons, they developed into rural service centers and still fill that role.

Summerville reached this stage of main street development sometime around 1890. Figure 45, taken from a Sanborn map, indicates the nature of Summerville's main street in 1888: small buildings, sometimes doubled up on lots, with open spaces of

Building placement on a stage 2 main street, Summerville, 1888. Stage 2 main streets characteristically include many small buildings with open spaces between them. (Courtesy Sanborn Map Co., Inc.)

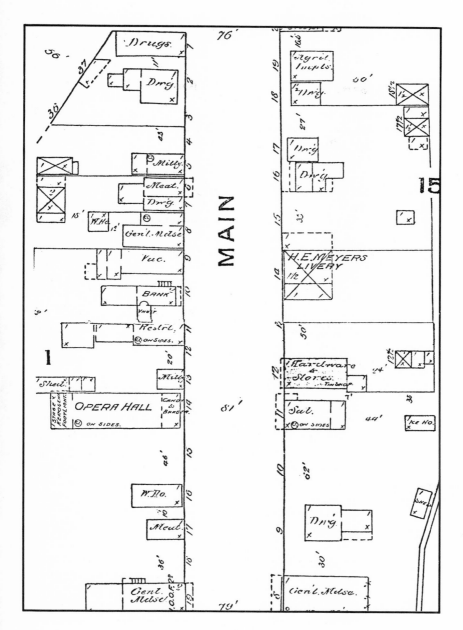

Fig. 45

MAIN

Drugs.

Drg.

Milly.

Meat.

Drg.

W.Ho.

Gen'l. Mdse.

Vac.

BANK

Restr.
Ⓛ ON SIDES.

Shed

Milly.

STAGE KEROSENE FOOTLIGHT

OPERA HALL
Ⓛ ON SIDES.

CAND & BAKERY

W.Ho.

Meat.

Gen'l. Mdse.

I.O.O.F.

1

Agril. Impls.

Drg.

Drg.

Drg.

H.E.MEYERS LIVERY

Hardware & Stores.
TIN SHOP.

Sal.
Ⓛ ON SIDES

Ice Ho.

Drg.

Shed

Gen'l. Mdse.

15

76'

50'

45'

81'

79'

107

irregular widths between them. Summerville's population in 1890 was 280.

Towns founded after Summerville arrived at the same stage of development later but developed comparable main streets. Halfway, for instance, was founded in 1907, nearly 20 years after Summerville's main street had reached stage 2, yet it developed a similar main street; so did Flora. Flora's main street stands deserted today but the main streets of Halfway and Imbler are still active. Figure 46 shows Halfway's prosperous stage 2 main street in 1976.

Towns with stage 2 main streets are remarkably similar. Their peak population varied by only 150 people. They had comparable economic bases. Their main streets looked much alike. Since these towns' early years their fates have differed, but the fundamental character of their main streets remains much the same.

Stage 3 Main Streets

Stage 3 main streets occurred in towns with economies based on some form of industry as well as on the provision of goods and services to the immediately surrounding area. These towns were linked with the regional economy and, to some degree, the national economy.

Main streets of this stage were lined by buildings that filled the street frontage but did not extend to a lot's full depth. Little open space remained between these buildings, which were becoming increasingly substantial. New buildings generally stood two stories high and they were likely to be brick, although a few frame structures continued to be built. By stage 3, main streets began to look like those typical of large towns. And in fact, these towns were larger than those with stage 2 streets. Their peak populations ranged from 450 to 1,000 people, many of whom were employed by local industries such as a lumber company or the railroad.

The Sanborn map of Huntington in 1911 (**fig. 47**) presents a well-developed stage 3 main street. The buildings present a solid front to the street but do not extend back to the mid-block alley. A railroad town, Huntington had a one-sided main street facing the tracks. The map includes a number of features indicative of

Fig. 46

Stage 2 main street, Halfway, 1976. The buildings along stage 2 main streets are still characteristically of wood construction and the street frontage continues to include open areas. Although the wares offered by stores that line stage 2 main streets have changed since the late 1800s—Halfway's current selection includes auto parts, chain saws, and television sets—the merchants are actually selling modern equivalents to turn-of-the-century goods. These small towns still fulfill the role of providing the rural population with basic supplies and services. (B. R. Bailey)

stage 3 main streets and the kind of regional economy that supported a stage 3 town. The park was installed at the insistence of the ladies of Huntington and the pagoda in Washington Street was used for band concerts. The depot was combined with a hotel, and the platform beyond was used for loading North Powder ice into refrigerator cars (probably for Snake River fruit brought into Huntington by the Northwestern Railroad). The hotel (for rail passengers), the ice and fruit businesses, and the short local rail lines, all elements of the regional economy at the time, subsequently failed and were never revived or replaced.

Figure 48 is a photograph of Huntington taken shortly after 1911. The block on the Sanborn map (**fig. 47**) appears in the

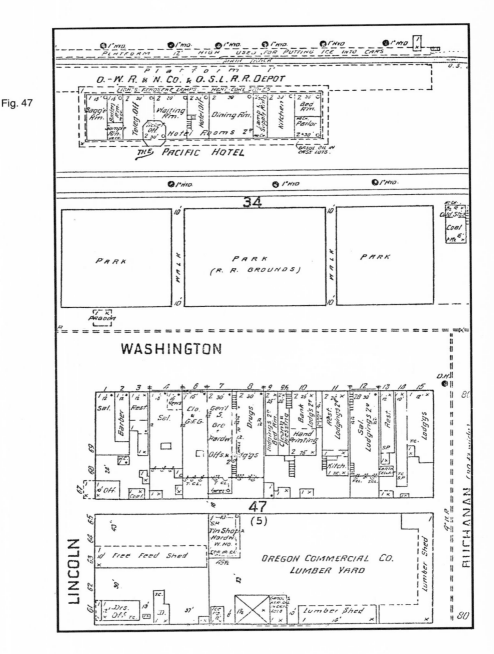

Fig. 47

110

center of the photograph. Of the two buildings under construction at the left, one is of brick and the other of wood, indicating that frame construction persisted even at this stage of main street development. This frame building is analogous to those on the main streets of Halfway and Flora, built at about the same time.

Figure 49, a photograph of Joseph, was taken in 1917. It presents another stage 3 main street. The buildings, lower than those in Huntington but as closely placed, are constructed of brick and concrete as well as wood. Initially, Joseph derived its support from the prosperous grain and stock district surrounding it, but after the railroad reached the town a lumber mill opened and supplemented the town's economy. Huntington and Joseph illustrate the variety of characteristics that can signify stage 3 main street development. Of the two, Joseph is the more typical; in its development, Huntington actually approaches stage 4.

With densely built-up main streets, whose wooden structures were being replaced by more expensive and durable brick, stone and concrete buildings, these towns' physical appearance reflected their relative prosperity and greater regional roles.

Stage 4 Main Streets

Stage 4 towns had main streets lined with numerous two-story brick buildings, many of which completely filled their lots. Several blocks may have been solidly packed with brick buildings. As a whole, however, the main street showed variety in the height, materials and lot depth of the buildings lining it. Despite this variety, records of stage 4 main streets reveal a consistently higher skyline and denser pattern of ground use than those in towns of the preceding stage.

Northeastern Oregon's largest towns all developed stage 4 main streets. All rapid-growth towns, they emerged as among the largest in the region within 15 years of their founding, at

Building placement on a stage 3 main street, Huntington, 1911. Spaces between the buildings largely have disappeared but the buildings still do not utilize the full depth of their lots. (Courtesy Sanborn Map Co., Inc.)

Fig. 48

Stage 3 main street, Huntington, about 1911. (The block in the preceding map is at the center of this photograph.) Huntington boomed in its early years and most of its construction was completed by 1895. Since this photograph was taken, little construction, replacement or facade modification has occurred. (OHS neg. 49117)

their peak housing between 1,000 and 2,000 people. Each served an area larger than its immediate environs. Enterprise and Union thrived as county seats. Elgin prospered as the railhead for Wallowa County. Sumpter served a large gold-mining district.

As the towns grew, their main streets progressed quickly through the first three stages of main street development. It was actually possible to see characteristics of all stages at the same time along these streets as they shifted from one to the next. Figures 50-54 are from Sanborn Company maps of Enterprise's main street in 1890, 1900, 1910, 1917 and 1923. The blocks included here were not the principal main street blocks, adjacent to the courthouse, but the next set west; the two sides of the street developed at different rates, reaching stage 3 on the north

Fig. 49

Stage 3 main street, Joseph, 1917. Most of Joseph's main street was built after 1900. The town's growth, based on the development of agriculture and the lumber industry, was slower than that of Huntington's, and its main street's building height and density is more typically stage 3 than Huntington's. Joseph's main street buildings have some of the most elaborate brickwork in the region; note the fasciae on the buildings in the left foreground and the front of the two-story building farther down the street. (OHS neg. 16043)

side and stage 4 on the south. In all towns, main street could reach its final form only when growth and the format of the town had stabilized. In an environment of constant change, as in Enterprise, the earlier stages developed incompletely before they were superseded.

Two stage 4 main streets appear in figures 55 and 56. The former shows the main street of Enterprise, about 1924. The block depicted in figures 50-54 lies beyond the tall, white bank building at right in the middle distance. Within a few years of this photograph, the last false-front buildings would be replaced by brick buildings and Enterprise's main street would be lined

Fig. 50

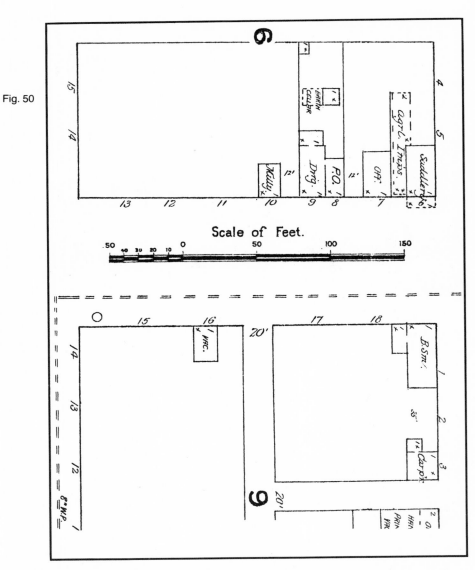

Enterprise, 1890. The street has reached stage 2 on the north side and stage 1 on the south. Note the types of businesses that line it. The principal main street blocks (seen in fig. 55) are the pair to the right of these. (Courtesy Sanborn Map Co., Inc.)

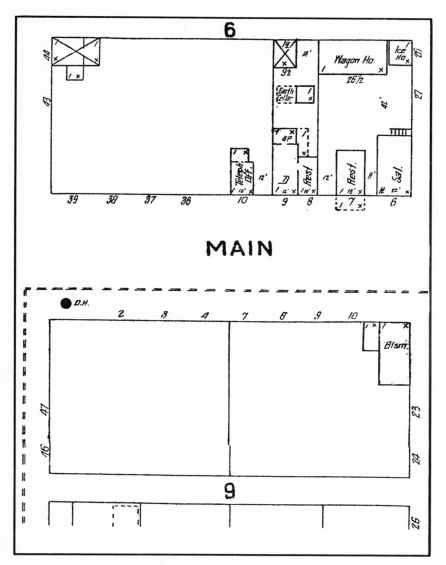

Fig. 51

Enterprise, 1900. The street is still at stage 2 on the north side and stage 1 on the south. However, a change in the building's uses indicates the displacement of businesses found on a stage 2 street. (Courtesy Sanborn Map Co., Inc.)

115

Fig. 52

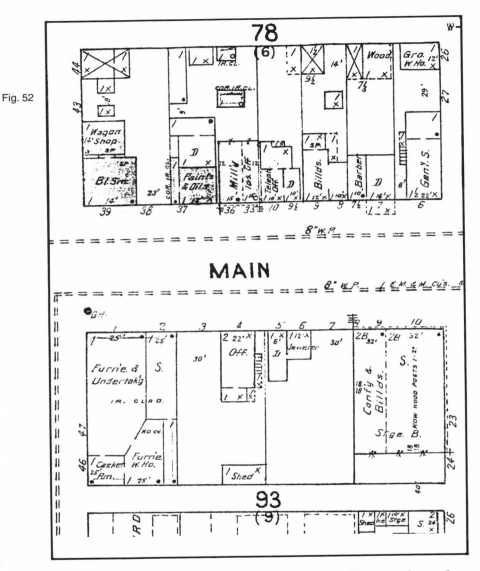

Enterprise, 1910. The north side of the street is trending toward stage 3 while the south side has a few new buildings characteristic of a stage 2 street and others characteristic of a stage 4. "D" indicates domestic quarters, still on both sides of the street. (Courtesy Sanborn Map Co., Inc.)

116

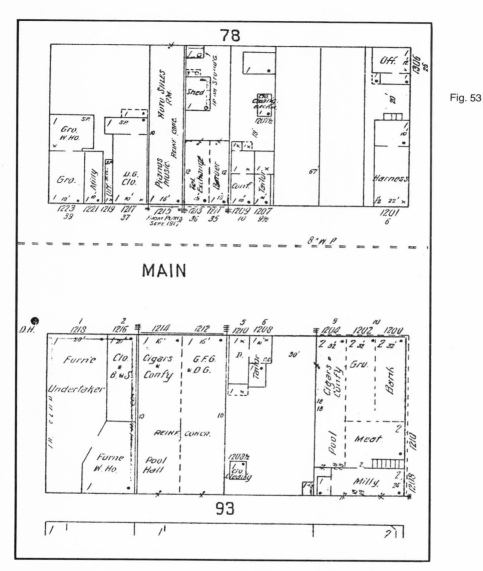

Fig. 53

Enterprise, 1917. The street's north side shows little change since 1910 but its south side, with new concrete buildings, increased shop density and further commercial specialization, now is nearly a stage 4 main street. (Courtesy Sanborn Map Co., Inc.)

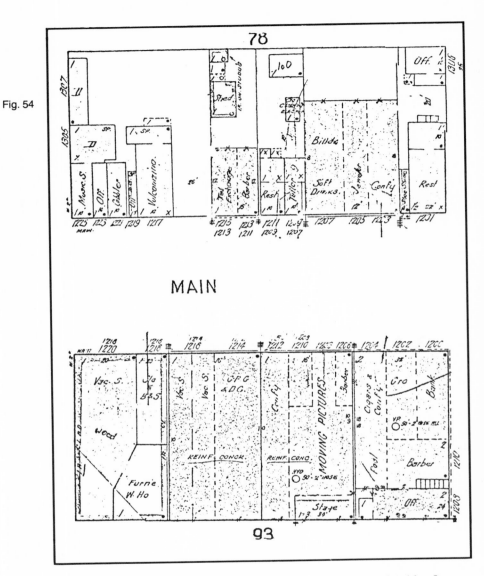

Fig. 54

Enterprise, 1923. The north side of the street now is at stage 3 (with a few stage 2 characteristics) but the south side has become solidly stage 4; a moving picture theater has filled the last vacant space on this block. (Courtesy Sanborn Map Co., Inc.)

118

Fig. 55

Stage 4 main street, Enterprise, about 1924. The blocks depicted in figures 50-54 are beyond the white bank building halfway down the street on the right; the false fronts remaining in the street's original business district soon would be replaced by brick and stone buildings similar to the foreground structures. With their increased building height, depth and density, stage 4 main streets often could not accommodate the continuing demand for main street space. As a result, the business district then expanded farther down the street or onto adjacent cross streets. (OHS neg. 15348)

completely with brick, stone, or reinforced concrete structures, many of which utilized the full depth of their lots. The business demand for street frontage was so great in this town that the main street business district expanded from its standard two-block length to almost four blocks.

Figure 56 is a photograph of Sumpter in 1903, taken from the hills west of the town, looking east. It shows Sumpter at the time of its greatest development. The hills to the east have been cleared to supply the wood-burning, lumber-hauling Sumpter Valley Railway. The long roofs on the far right side of the town cover the depot and associated warehouses. Most of the residen-

Fig. 56

Stage 4 main street, Sumpter, 1903. In this photograph, main street crosses town from left to right (most of the residential district is off to the left). The main street and its cross streets are lined by a dense jumble of large buildings. This main street bears little resemblance to Elgin's stage 1 main street pictured in figure 44. (Courtesy Oregon Collection, University of Oregon)

tial district is to the left, off the photograph. Sumpter's main street crosses the center of the photograph from left to right. It is lined by densely packed two-story buildings, most of which are wooden. The predominance of wood reflects the haste with which Sumpter was built. Within 10 years, however, many of these buildings were replaced by more substantial brick structures.

The business district of Sumpter, as with Enterprise, needed more main street frontage than that provided in the usual two-block area. Sumpter's restricted site and its highway alignment encouraged the expansion of the business district onto adjacent side streets. Sumpter, a large town with a well-developed main street, bears little resemblance to the pioneer Elgin of figure 44.

Summary

A number of new towns were platted in northeastern Oregon as the region was settled. Although founded for a variety of reasons—either to make money for their founders, or to serve passing traffic, or to supply surrounding districts—the underlying motive was always economic. Since most of a town's economic activity revolved around its main street business district, founders realized that their town's growth and prosperity depended on that street's development, and planned accordingly.

Thus, main street was the first part of a new town to develop. The earliest towns consisted of a row of commercial and domestic buildings along the main street (often, for financial reasons, both functions were under one roof). A few houses were scattered through the rest of the platted town; perhaps a church completed the new town. As the town grew, its main street filled in with more buildings. The nature of the buildings changed as the street evolved, showing a progression in style and materials. Town size, economic base and main street character were linked, and each stage of main street development reflected distinct steps in the town's growth.

In northeastern Oregon, towns grew rapidly in their early years and during that time their main streets showed the greatest rate of change. When town growth ceased, main street development slowed and the street's character changed little thereafter. The few new buildings that were built later tended to be smaller than the older buildings. In a sense, the development sequence reversed and the streets began to retrace their steps. Of this, more later.

The
Roles of
Main Street ___

V

THE PRIMARY ROLES of main street were economic and social. The economic role is usually emphasized, but the social role, although less extensively documented, is equally important. The level of main street activity is determined by the health and scale of a town's economic base. All northeastern Oregon towns experienced a period of relative prosperity, corresponding to the period of peak construction along main streets. An assessment of these towns' actual prosperity will indicate whether the degree to which northeastern Oregon's main streets were developed was economically justified.

The social function of main street has shown more constancy than its economic one. Like the economic role, however, in many of the small towns it has been affected by the population decline. Small-town main streets provided the setting for social activity. With the decline in population, formal main street activities have become infrequent. Informal activities persist, indicating that these streets fulfill fundamental social needs.

The Economic Role of Main Street

The economic role of a main street is perhaps its most definitive one. In certain respects the social role is governed by it: a main street's financial activites draw people to it; when people collect the social role unfolds. Business enterprises accounted for the construction of most of the buildings along main street, and provided the occupants for them.

An analysis of the economic role is a two-part process. First, the street's economic structure must be identified. Then the prosperity of the street must be determined. Identification of

123

Fig. 57

Main street business establishment interiors typically photographed as evidence of a town's economic health included dry goods and general stores, banks and saloons. Interior photographs of stores displayed the economic backbone of main street while views inside banks provided proof of prosperity; saloon interior shots portrayed some of the social pleasures associated with towns. The owner of this successful store in Elgin, L. A. Stoop, leans leisurely against the cash register. In 1912 his wares most prominently displayed included seeds, brooms and laundry soap, canned fish, Karo, Red Cross coffee, Golden Rod oats and Tree tea. (OHS neg. 63323)

Bank interior shots (fig. 58) always showed men formally posed at tellers' windows. The footrests indicate a leisurely pace. Those who entered the bank could immediately perceive the banking business heirarchy, demonstrated by the progression of offices starting at the teller's window, then the bookkeeper's office, and finally the imposing "Director's" door. (OHS neg. 63327)

This Sumpter saloon (fig. 59) may have been the fanciest in all of northeastern Oregon, for it was in one of the region's wealthiest and most firmly established mining towns. A collection of good cigars, spittoons under the footrail, and a cast-iron stove hint at the conveniences promoting lively and convivial nightlife. (OHS neg. 1642)

124

Fig. 58

Fig. 59

125

economic structure requires knowledge of the main street's businesses, how they differed from those of other towns, and how they changed with time. Sanborn Company maps provide essential spatial information about the buildings and the businesses they housed. Main street business prosperity is evaluated to determine whether the street's physical development had a sound financial base. The extent to which a street was developed may have been justified by local financial resources. Sometimes, though, the street's development exceeded the area's ability to support it, and in these cases, apparent prosperity was followed by failure.

Few business records from the period of town founding have survived; those that exist are often found strictly by chance. Prosperity must therefore by analyzed by other means: business directories and Sanborn maps. The directories document changes due to expansion, contraction and migration within the business communities of selected towns. Immigration and emigration rates are closely examined, to determine their connection with main street construction, as revealed by the Sanborn maps. In this way, mobility and economic stability in the business communities can be related to the types of buildings that were built along main streets.

Main Street Economic Structure

As demonstrated, a town's size, its economic base and its regional role are connected and their effect on main street's physical development has been discussed. These factors also have some bearing on the specific business activities that occur along the main street.

Each of the three final stages of main street development is associated with a distinctive array of financial ventures. Thus,

---

Land use on a stage 2 main street, Richland, 1911. Stage 2 main streets were unspecialized business streets with commercial, residential and light manufacturing functions. In Richland, a road leading to the south had several commercial buildings along it (see fig. 35). Such T- or L-shaped business districts were unusual in the region. (Courtesy Sanborn Map Co., Inc.)

126

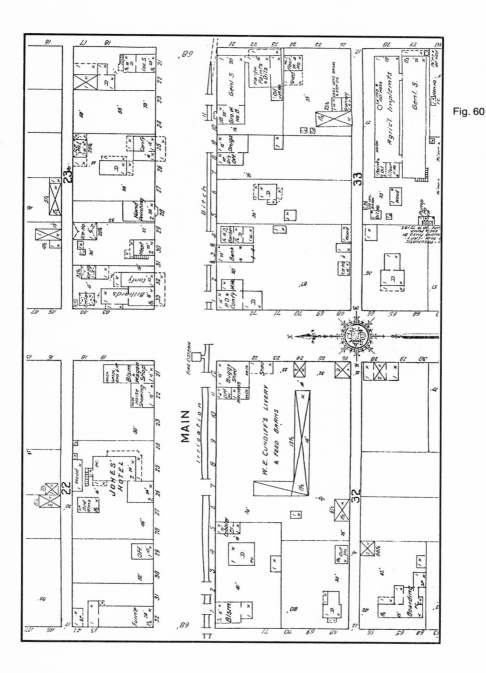

Fig. 60

127

the progression from stage 2 to stage 4 is accompanied not only by an evolution in the buildings' physical appearance, but also by a shift in the activities within them. In general, buildings along stage 2 main streets hosted a wide variety of basic economic activities while those along stage 4 main streets, predominantly commercial in nature, were more specialized. Towns with a unique regional role or economic base often had distinctive groups of activities located along their main streets.

Small towns and large cities have many common characteristics, one being the basic activities that occur in them. In large cities, however, these activities occur in separate locations; there are residential districts, commercial districts and industrial zones. In small towns, on the other hand, the activities are often mixed. In northeastern Oregon's stage 2 towns, for example, houses, businesses and small industrial establishments often stood side by side along the main street.

As northeastern Oregon's towns progressed through the stages of development, the role of their main streets grew more specialized. This was due to two trends. First was the emergence of main street as an area of retail shops; the houses and small industries disappeared and main street became principally a commercial center. The trend that followed corresponded to the decline of small-town main streets as a place of business. During the 1920s Baker and La Grande, as northeastern Oregon's largest cities, began to absorb much of the business on which the smaller towns' main streets depended.

Stage 2 Main Streets

Figure 60, from the 1911 Sanborn map of Richland, presents a typical stage 2 main street, which was characterized by a mixture of open space, homes and businesses. Basic needs of the surrounding community were easily met by the businesses along the streets. The list of stores in all stage 2 towns includes at least one general store, a drugstore, a meat store and a hardware store. By 1910, each small town also had a bank and a weekly newspaper, which was printed in its main street headquarters. Men tended to socialize at the barber's, saloon, billiards hall or lodge hall, and women and children at the confectionery.

128

The agricultural orientation of the stage 2 town is indicated by the presence of at least one blacksmith and a place selling "agricultural implements" (farm equipment). Livery stables and stage barns, evidence of the town's link with the regional transportation network, always stood on main street, often with wagon and harness shops nearby.

Main street also provided for the needs of both the transient and the permanent resident. Travelers lodged at main street hotels, which also took more permanent boarders. Houses were interspersed among the shops; some of the latter had small domestic quarters attached.

Main street at this stage was an area in which to live, shop, bank, socialize and work as a shopkeeper or tradesperson. All of these activities occurred along main street in towns with populations of 400 or less. This mingling of residential, commercial and light industrial functions occurred as long as a town remained in stage 2, sometimes over a long time span. The role of the town might change, but the mixture of activities continued.

Stage 3 Main Streets

As towns grew, the range of activities along their main streets narrowed. Stage 3 towns saw a reduction in the number of domestic and light industrial establishments. Although a few houses still stood along main street, most of the people who resided there lived in the upstairs of new two-story buildings. Sometimes they were lodgers but more often they were shopkeepers, living above their stores. By this time, agricultural implements were no longer sold on main street and the livery stables and blacksmith shops had been nudged farther down the street, or off it entirely.

Stage 4 Main Streets

The trend toward commercial specialization intensified on stage 4 streets. The ranks of stores commonly found in stage 2 towns (general, drug, meat and hardware stores) were amplified while tradespeople were displaced; carpentry shops disappeared and blacksmiths relocated. Many general stores now lined the streets and they were joined by a number of more specialized stores such as those selling furniture, paint, wallpaper and jewelry. Establishments offering specialized services increased in number. Stage 4 main streets had milliners, photographers and laundries, restaurants and confectioneries became more common and dance halls and opera houses supplemented the entertainment provided in lodge halls.

The more developed main streets had something else that those of most smaller towns did not: professional offices. Some offices were in single-story buildings but often they occupied the second floor of the two-story business blocks typical of stage 4 main streets. The offices on ground floors were usually insurance and doctors' offices; the latter also frequently occupied second-floor offices in two-story buildings, along with lawyers. Residential use of the second floor almost ceased. Shopkeepers lived elsewhere and many persons roomed in boarding houses on side streets or in the new, large hotels.

Stage 4 main streets resembled those of much larger towns and cities. They were lined with commercial and service establishments; residences and light industry had disappeared. The relationship of land use to stages of main street development is portrayed in figures 50-54, the maps of a block in Enterprise from 1890 to 1923.

Main Streets in Railroad and Mining Towns

Along the main streets of towns with a specialized economic base another, distinct, group of activities sometimes emerged. These were the towns that drew a large population of single males. The main streets of Huntington, a railroad town, and Sumpter, a mining town, contained businesses that catered to these men. As figure 47 indicates, the main street of Huntington was lined with saloons, restaurants and second-floor lodgings.

The main street of Sumpter served a large town that included both families and many single men. It was two and a half blocks long with businesses also located on the cross streets that led to the depot, to Baker to the east, or to other mining towns to the west. The northern end of main street served the general population, with conventional types of businesses such as dry goods

Fig. 61

Granite Street, Sumpter, about 1905. The use of each building in this photograph can be guessed simply by looking at it. With its shingled, gabled roof paralleling the street and its front porch, the Star Hotel's domestic character is typical of early main street hotels. The false fronts next door embellish small, narrow buildings usually occupied by low-profit, high-turnover businesses such as saloons, cigar stores and barber-shops. Beyond stands the most ornate structure in Sumpter: a bank. Another gabled roof beyond the bank belongs to a boarding house which, judging by its set-back from the street, probably was built as a private home. The large white building farther up the street is a typical general store with second floor residential quarters.

Sumpter's main street was the supply depot for many mining towns in the Blue Mountains, and, as a through highway, much heavy mining equipment moved along it. Here a sixteen-horse team pulls a water wagon (another six horses are hitched behind to help brake the wagon when going downhill). (OHS neg. 51202)

and clothing stores, a butcher and a drugstore and around the corners a furniture store, several groceries and a confectionery. The southerly blocks however (shown in **fig. 62**), contained seven saloons and two hotels in addition to the bank and general

131

store, and around the corner behind the saloons were a dance hall and a number of "female boarding houses." The Sanborn maps of the main streets of Huntington and Sumpter provide evidence that the colorful legends surrounding main streets in mining and railroad towns had some basis in reality.

Modern Replacements

The types of businesses along northeastern Oregon's main streets changed as times changed. However, most only represented modern replacements that fulfilled the same needs as their outdated counterparts. Food and clothing continued to be supplied, of course, although in the larger towns these articles were sold in markets and department stores instead of in general and dry goods stores. Gas stations and garages replaced the livery stables and blacksmiths' shops in the 1920s and the tavern and cafe replaced the saloon and confectionery. Photographers' shops appeared along main street just long enough to note their existence; as camera ownership became more widespread they disappeared, superseded by the drugstore with its stock of films and "Kodaks." Millinery shops disappeared in the 1920s when women began to bob their hair, to be replaced much later by the beauty parlor. One curious main street facility disappeared entirely from the region: bathtubs in the back of barber shops for use by sheepherders when they came into town.

Economic Structure: Summary

The first 50 years of town founding, 1865-1915, saw main streets develop and become increasingly specialized. The small-town main street had many kinds of activities along it, commercial, residential and light industrial in nature. As towns grew, houses and tradespersons' establishments were displaced by increasing numbers of stores. The main street evolved into a street

Land use on a specialized stage 4 main street, Sumpter, 1900. These are the blocks that appear on the right half of figure 56. While the upper end of Sumpter's main street served the general public, this end served the miners. (Courtesy Sanborn Map Co., Inc.)

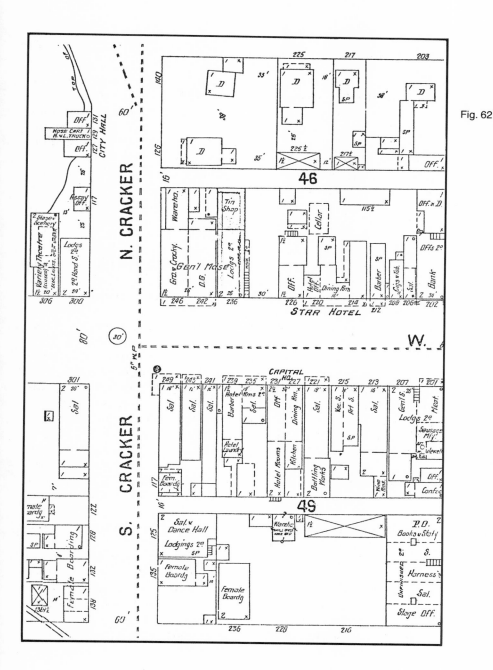

Fig. 62

lined by shops and offices offering specialized goods and services.

The physical development of a main street, characterized by increasing building density, was accompanied by an evolution in the types of economic activities found along the street. Activities that encompassed adjacent open space, such as residences and stables, gave way to more specialized enterprises that generated higher business returns in less space. It is clear that as main streets developed, the types of buildings and types of businesses inside those structures changed.

Main Street Prosperity

The building of a main street represents a sizable investment of enthusiasm, energy and capital. Construction of northeastern Oregon's main streets was largely completed by 1910 or 1920. The stimulus for construction was the region's settlement and its economic development. The new towns attracted businessmen who, quickly erecting a row of buildings, established the main street.

Whether or not the new main streets were prosperous is questionable. Each town's local population, although growing, was still relatively small, and each main street had a number of competitors. Some streets did develop into more elaborate districts but this development did not necessarily reflect local business prosperity. It may have resulted from outsiders who, coming in with fresh capital, artificially stimulated main street development. It is possible, in fact, that some main streets were not at all independently prosperous and that their physical development was actually financed with money brought into the town by new arrivals.

Unfortunately, sources are not readily available to resolve the question of prosperity. Old business records have been lost or dispersed. Building permit procedures were begun after the streets were built, complicating the identification of builders and construction costs. Loans or other transactions relating to the financing of the buildings were only occasionally recorded with the county clerk and if they were, they went into the deeds register, which is not indexed. Therefore, less direct methods must be employed to determine whether northeastern Oregon's main street business communities prospered and could have financed their own construction.

Business Community Size and Stability

It is assumed that the size of a business community reflects the businessmen's perception of the town's potential, and thus that if the business community grew, it was because businessmen thought they could make a living in the town. It is also assumed that the length of these persons' stay in the town reflects the success of their expectations. If a town were indeed a good place in which to operate a business, the businessmen would stay there. If, on the other hand, they couldn't support themselves satisfactorily, they would sell out and move on. Size and stability of a business community, and the persistence of its members, can be used to determine perceived versus real prosperity. A business community with a low turnover rate would indicate satisfactory returns; conversely, a high turnover rate in the community would suggest inadequate returns compensated by a continual influx of new enthusiasm and capital.

Ten towns were selected for study: three each from stages 2, 3 and 4 of main street development plus a fourth, a more specialized stage 4 town. (Stage 1 towns are not included because this was a transitory stage of development; most surviving towns quickly progressed beyond it. Only a few of those that lingered in stage 1 survived past 1915, and because of their small size they did not receive detailed coverage in the business directories.) These ten towns were chosen according to several criteria: they received adequate business directory coverage, possessed a representative variety of economic bases and comprised a group that was widely distributed throughout the counties and the region. Sumpter, the tenth town, has been included to provide an example of a gold-rush community, but because of this unique character is not included in the general discussion that follows.

Business directories published in 1873, 1881, 1891, 1901, 1913 and 1923 were used to identify the members of the towns' business communities. Bradstreet's Commercial Ratings for 1926 and 1932 extend the coverage but there is some discrepancy between the two listing systems. Each town's business listings were compared from one directory to the next. In the ten towns studied, a total of 2,112 individuals were identified as businessmen and analyzed for their persistence in the business community.*

The results of this analysis appear in table 10. The total number of names in each business community was derived from the business directories. In a given directory, the "old" names are those repeated from the previous directory listing. Once this number of names common to both directories was established, the numbers of "new" and "gone" names could be determined. "New" names (those that did not appear in the previous directory) were derived by subtracting the "old" names from the directory's total. "Gone" names for a business directory were those that had disappeared since the previous directory; this total was determined by subtracting the "old" names from the previous directory's total. The table indicates that a town's classification as stage 2, 3, or 4 is roughly correlated with the total number of businesses in the town during the years surveyed.

Main Street Immigration

Among the ten towns, growth patterns varied by town size and function. All of the towns experienced a rapid influx of businessmen shortly after they began to develop, which (as has been discussed) accounted for the rapid sale of main street lots and the quick construction of stage 1 and 2 main streets. The time between town founding and the first business directory listing varied so the size of the first business community recorded often reflected the town's age as well as its growth. For some of the towns, particularly the smaller ones, the initial influx established the basic size of the community. In the larger towns, however,

---

*Listings were scanned to exclude the people identified as ranchers and to avoid counting listings twice. Civil employees such as notaries, sheriffs, judges and postmasters were included because the positions were often short-term and the individuals who occupied them left their more permanent private businesses only temporarily.

early growth was more rapid and the period of growth lasted longer, bringing in more members and intensifying main street activity. The railroad and mining towns of Huntington and Sumpter respectively, stand out in this group as larger towns with an especially compressed growth period. Within a few years of founding they possessed relatively large business communities; shortly thereafter, however, these declined in size.

Main Street Immigration and Emigration

The maintenance or growth of a business community does not necessarily signify economic well-being along main street. In the 10 towns surveyed, few names were carried over from one period to the next in the business directories. In fact there was an 80- to 90-percent turnover rate in most of these towns in their early years. The high turnover rate explains why city fathers advertised the advantages of their towns so vigorously; the size of the business community could be maintained or increased only by attracting new members. The failure of Flora was due not so much to the departure of its first group of businessmen as to a failure to recruit replacements.

Table 11 presents one explanation for the high turnover rate in the towns' early business communities. The table presents simple ratios: the number of residents per businessman.* A simple, straightforward measure, the ratio does not take into ac-

---

*The towns analyzed are the same as in table 10, excluding Sumpter. The ratios are derived by dividing population by the number of businessmen. For the town figures, the town's population is divided by the number of businessmen in the town. The same process is followed for hinterland ratios: rural population divided by the number of businessmen in town. The hinterland population is the total population of the contiguous precincts that looked to the town for their needs. Stage 2 towns drew only from their host precincts while stage 3 towns typically had at least one adjacent precinct which, lacking a town, looked to these. Stage 4 towns drew from a larger hinterland, often encompassing two or three precincts. Enterprise, as a county seat, served the entire county but nonetheless, the hinterland is still considered to be only the adjoining rural precincts whose roads led to it rather than to another town.

count what types of businesses were present and it sidesteps assumptions about the number of people required to support particular types of stores. It is useful, however, when trying to understand the general support level for main streets.

A comparison of the three groups of towns reveals differences between the towns as well as general changes through time. The themes that emerge from the table relate to main street prosperity and the changing relationships of stage 2, 3 and 4 towns. The table shows that the towns became more alike in some ways and less alike in others, and it helps explain the ways in which business districts failed or persisted.

The ratios indicate that early in each of the towns' histories relatively few people supported their main street. As towns grew this changed but those that remained in stage 2 continued to hold relatively few residents per businessman. When this was the case, the towns apparently contained only the businessmen, their immediate families, and few others (normally towns also hold the families of people who work for wages). Hired by the proprietors of main street, wage earners worked as clerks (in stores), waiters (in saloons and hotels), apprentices (in trades such as carpentry and blacksmithing) and hired hands (in livery stables or railyards). A town occupied primarily by businessmen and their families was a town of lean profit margins, with business volumes too low to require and support many supplementary people.

Stage 3 main streets were supported by slightly more townfolk per businessman than the stage 2 main streets. Those of stage 3 developed in towns with some form of industry that provided employment off of main street. If the support industries failed in a stage 3 town, it meant hard times for merchants because their business district lacked an adequate underlying rural support base.

Stage 4 towns were more broadly based than their smaller neighbors, with industrial employment in town, populous rural hinterlands, and regional roles that extended beyond their immediate area. Similarly to stage 2 and 3 towns, stage 4 towns struggled in their early years because of weak town and rural support. Once established, however, their main streets were sup-

138

ported by more town residents than either of the other two groups of towns. The apparently poor rural support ratio in table 11 is misleading. The ratio is due more to the large size of the business district than to low rural populations. The larger regional role of stage 4 towns meant that their business districts were based on populations that extended beyond their immediate rural hinterland. Thus, their adjacent rural population was a relatively less important factor in main street prosperity.

By the end of the 60 years covered in table 11, all towns had higher support ratios than they began with. The later, more favorable, balances were reached by a reduction in the numbers of businessmen at the same time that populations continued to increase. In other words, the early main streets were simply too large for their support base and there was a high failure rate.

Times must have been difficult for merchants in the first decades of a town's existence. The year 1890 shows up as a particularly unfavorable time. While this might be an artificial impression (caused perhaps by a more complete directory coverage that year of businessmen who were not included in earlier and later directories), it may be that in fact, relatively more people were trying to earn their living in main street activities at that time than at any other.

The biggest jump in support for main street businesses occurred between 1900 and 1910. The doubling of the ratios (even more in the smallest towns) resulted from a halving of the number of businessmen in the towns. This reduction seems to have been the consequence of partnership dissolutions and the subsequent disappearance of the junior partner as an entrepreneur. The number of actual business establishments along the streets remained constant or even increased, as documented by the Sanborn maps. The reduction in the number of main street entrepreneurs resulted in greater prosperity for those who remained, as evidenced by the number of well-built structures erected along the main streets between 1900 and 1910.

By 1930, the ratios of town folk to businessmen became more similar in towns of all sizes. Town sizes and business district relationships have been thoroughly analyzed in modern towns but the relationships were very different in the volatile period of town founding and early settlement. The lopsided ratios in the early decades reflect main streets that were too large for the population on hand. A more favorable balance was eventually established but it took many decades and was essentially based on high turnover rates and frequent business failures.

The factors behind the increased similarity in the town resident to businessman ratios in the 1930s are incompletely understood but might represent the increased integration of the town networks. Improved roads and greater mobility, especially in the 1920s, meant that small towns lost the competitive advantage of proximity to rural customers and competed more directly with the larger towns. The small towns, now integrated with the larger towns, developed comparable ratios of townfolk to businessmen.

While towns were becoming more similar internally, they diverged with respect to their hinterlands. The smallest towns always had a relatively large rural support base for their main streets. The stage 2 main streets began to fail in the 1920s. The tremendous upsurge in the rural ratio for stage 2 main streets was the result of the business failure of many of their members. Their surrounding rural populations, increasingly mobile, turned to other towns for their needs, probably to stage 4 towns. Thus the business districts of the larger towns served an ever-larger rural area and population.

Tables 10 and 11 trace the towns of northeastern Oregon from their optimistic but shaky beginnings through periods of expansion, stability and decline. Business district expansion required high recruitment for the districts were unstable internally and had a high turnover rate. Table 10 substantiates the high turnover rate and table 11 indicates some of the reasons for it. Poor early support for the towns stressed their merchants and although some equilibrium was reached, the main streets were not the stable, prosperous places romanticized today.

Improved mobility after 1910 tied the towns more closely together and exposed the smaller towns to new levels of competition. Unable to compete, many of the smallest towns eventually lost their business districts. Towns intermediate in size prospered and grew beyond stage 2 but their industrial base was narrow and uncertain, resulting in instability along their main streets. The largest towns, with large and broad economic bases, managed to hold their own and even prosper in the face of neighboring towns' failures.

Main Street Emigration

By 1920, the number of businessmen had increased again. During the next decade recruitment fell so far behind emigration that the total number of people in business for themselves in 1930 was less than it had been in 1890. Rural and town populations both declined by 1930, which made the towns less desirable places in which to locate or start up a new business. It is interesting to note that despite these discouraging trends, the number of businessmen who stayed on in the towns between 1920 and 1930 was about the same as in the preceding periods of growth.

Size and Stability: Summary

The earliest of northeastern Oregon's main streets, those of the 1870s, prospered, but overexpansion along the many new main streets of the next decade caused a high turnover rate among main street businessmen. The high rate of recruitment and replacement in the 1880s and 1890s suggests, however, that the streets continued to seem attractive enough as business locations. Town and hinterland populations continued to increase after 1900 but business community recruitment began to lag. The total number of people in business along main streets declined. Between 1890 and 1920, regional business communities experienced no overall change in size, although the population served by the towns increased substantially.

The high turnover rate typical of all of the main streets examined probably resulted from a variety of decisions and ambitions. It can be construed as evidence of short-lived speculative undertakings: early businessmen established themselves in a town, developed it a bit, and sold out at a profit. However, it is likely that the high turnover rate more often represented failure than profit taking.

Prosperity and Main Street Construction

Most construction along main street occurred during the first 20 years of a town's existence, the principal period of its business community's expansion. These 20 years, then, were critical in determining the nature of its main street. Since most of the early construction was financed by capital brought in by newcomers, it tended to reflect the financiers' past successes (on which expectations were based), rather than on the actual prosperity of the town's business community. The high turnover rate suggests that these early expectations were not often met.

A main street's growth from stage 2 to stage 4 entailed the construction of a number of larger, more expensive buildings. While stage 2 streets were characterized by wood-frame buildings, often with false fronts, stage 4 main streets had two-story brick business blocks. Towns identified as stage 2 experienced a relatively brief period of main street construction, during which most of their original buildings were erected by newcomers and with imported capital. Few of these buildings would be replaced by newer or larger ones. Stage 3 and 4 towns, however, developed their main streets over a longer period, and these were more prosperous than stage 2 business districts. By the end of their construction period, most had succeeded in lowering the turnover rate. The importance of imported capital decreased. All of the main street businesses and buildings were locally owned, an increasing number of them by established business community members.

The physical appearance of a main street reflected to some degree the range of establishments located there. A greater variety of buildings appeared along stage 2 main streets than along streets in stage 4. The former were lined by small business buildings, houses, livery barns, corrals, and sheds for storing farm equipment. The latter, with more specialized main streets, had buildings that were designed for more specific commercial functions. It is interesting to examine the types of businesses that probably generated the earnings necessary to erect the large buildings typical of the larger towns.

Business Persistence and Type of Business

Business communities along stage 2 main streets generally experienced a high turnover rate. Usually, however, a few businessmen stayed on. Presumably, these were the more prosperous businessmen, satisfied with their profits. Stage 3 and 4 main streets were built by relatively stable commercial communities. Prosperous and persistent businessmen played a particularly important part in determining the character of stage 3 and 4 main streets, for their establishments eventually constituted a large portion of the business district. To better understand their influence, it is helpful to look first at the total array of main street businesses in the region and identify which of them had the most stable ownership.

A summation (based on 1910 and 1911 Sanborn maps) of the business enterprises along eight northeastern Oregon main streets is presented in table 12. All of the towns in table 10 are included except Sumpter and Flora (the latter was never mapped by the Sanborn Company). Each of the businesses recorded here was distinct, and had main street frontage. The predominance of the general store is striking. Transportation-related activities were numerous and the total number of services located along main street was also comparatively high. The importance of the social role of the main street shows up in the frequency of gathering places: restaurants, confectioneries, saloons, and billiard and lodge halls.

Table 13 is a summary of business persistence in 1901, 1913 and 1923. Based on directory listings, the recurring names are grouped by business. For example, in 1901, 12 general store owners (among seven towns) had been in business since 1891. In 1913, 18 people with general stores had been listed in the same towns 11 years earlier. Even considering the differences in date and data sources, tables 12 and 13 graphically depict the high rate of flux along the main streets and also identify the businesses that showed the greatest stability. The general store merchant, druggist, banker, doctor and lawyer generally had the longest tenure. Other businesses commonly established along

143

main streets, such as butcher shops, saloons and barbers, experienced a consistently high turnover rate.

The persistence of the general store merchant, druggist and banker implies that their businesses were the most prosperous along main street. Bradstreet's Commercial Ratings indicates that in each town the general store had by far the largest assets and the best credit rating; they were sometimes part of a milling and mercantile company based in the town, the president of which frequently doubled as president of the local bank. Drugstores and furniture stores were others with high ratings.

The persistence and prominence of the general store, drugstore, furniture store and bank help to explain the character of many of main street's largest buildings. These were built and occupied by the largest and most profitable businesses in the town, while the smaller buildings, built as the town passed through stage 2, tended to house more transient renters. The large buildings accommodated large stocks and were an advertisement of the success of their owners. But the buildings represented more. The construction of a brick or stone building was widely publicized and the completed building was widely admired. Built later in a main street's development, usually with locally earned capital, a brick or stone business block symbolized the success not only of the merchants, but of the town itself.

The Social Role of Main Street

While the economic role of a main street was important, the social role of the street was equally significant. Men, women,

---

In 1900, Mr. L. A. Stoop of Elgin (hatless, with beer in hand) ran a successful saloon; at 10:45 A.M. business was well underway in this eclectically decorated establishment. Stoop was on his way up in the world, as evidenced by the establishment under his proprietorship twelve years later (fig. 64, following page) (perhaps due to inflation or increasing property taxes, rather than personal profit, the cost of whiskey rose from 10 to 12½ cents a pony during that time). If the number of inches around his waist was in direct proportion to his success, Stoop certainly flourished in the fifteen years between 1900 and 1915, when the exterior shot of his business was taken (fig. 65). (OHS negs. 37765, 54917 & 63324)

Fig. 63

145

Fig. 64

Fig. 65

Fig. 66

Next to Stoop's bar (note the striped pole in the exterior shot) was a barbershop and (through the door at the back) a laundry: "Notice: All Laundry Strictly Cash. When You Come For Your Laundry, Please Have the MONEY." Barbershops were socializing places. (OHS neg. 63328)

children, and the community as a whole, met on main street, brought together in both organized gatherings and spontaneous encounters. These social activities varied in their formality, location and intensity, but in all cases, people met people. At the turn of the century, face-to-face contact and live entertainment were the only means of conducting business and socializing, and main street was where most of it happened. The arrival of the telephone and radio altered patterns of contact, reducing the importance and frequency of centralized social activities, but the social role of the street persisted. Even today, main streets provide the setting for significant forms of entertainment and information exchange.

Almost any location along the main street could provide the setting for some form of interaction between people. Some activities were site specific, focused on one place, while others were more diffuse and street specific, using the entire length of the

Fig. 67

MAIN STREET SOCIAL PLACES AND ACTIVITIES

OLD MAIN STREETS

Site Specific		Street Specific	
Formal	Informal	Formal	Informal
MEN			
Lodge Halls	Saloons Stage Stops Post Offices General Stores	Parades	Sidewalk Strolls
WOMEN			
Lodge Halls	Confectioneries	Parades	Sidewalk Strolls
COMMUNITY			
Opera Houses Churches Schools	Opera Houses Churches Schools	Parades	Sidewalk Strolls

CONTEMPORARY MAIN STREETS

Site Specific		Street Specific	
Formal	Informal	Formal	Informal
MEN			
Lodge Halls	Cafes Taverns Post Offices Hardware Stores	Parades	Sidewalk Strolls
WOMEN			
Lodge Halls	Cafes Markets	Parades	Sidewalk Strolls
COMMUNITY			
Churches Schools	Churches Schools	Parades	Sidewalk Strolls

148

Fig. 68

Union High School, about 1920. Along with lodge halls and churches, schools were the most important centers of social activity in northeastern Oregon's small towns. With frequently scheduled events open to the public, schools in the vicinity of main street business districts increased the concentration of people along the streets' length. Main streets and high schools generally were the only completely public gathering places in a town. (OHS neg. 63329)

street. Exchanges indoors were site specific and were more commonly associated with certain kinds of businesses or organizations than with others. Most encounters were spontaneous and informal although some were organized, marked by formality and official rituals. There was a variety of popular businesses that provided the opportunity to stand around and trade news. Men and women tended to patronize different kinds of shops as they went about their daily business (see **fig. 67**). Men did much of their visiting in barber shops, saloons, post offices, banks and general stores. The diversity of stores where women lingered was less but included confectioneries, butcher shops, groceries and some general stores. The informal social exchanges along main street involving patrons and proprietors was important in

149

developing and maintaining a sense of community within the town.

The most highly organized and traditional activities revolved around the lodge halls and schools. In the larger towns, the Odd Fellows' lodges and Masonic temples usually stood two stories high on a prominent corner in the center of the business district, and their ground floors were usually occupied by either a general store, a post office, or some other busy center; the lodges were places of active participation in the town's daily business. Nighttime lodge hall meetings, on the second floor, extended the hours of building use and contributed to a nighttime bustle along main street.

Schools (see **fig. 68**) and churches were the other important institutional centers of social activity in small towns. In several northeastern Oregon towns, the churches and schools stood on the edge of the business district, while in others they were several blocks away. In either case, their proximity to main street contributed to its central importance, increasing the concentration of people along its length, thereby increasing social contact. Schools often scheduled events open to all community members. In fact, main streets and schools were generally the only two completely public gathering places in a town. Therefore, a school's location on or near main street meant that these two centers of community interaction could reinforce the importance of one another.

Main street provided the setting for much of a town's organized entertainment. Concerts held in main street bandstands were common. Old photographs, Sanborn maps and business directories indicate that around the turn of the century nearly every small town in the region supported a band. In the evening, opera houses and privately owned dance halls provided alternatives to scheduled lodge-hall activities. The entertainment offered in opera houses ranged from traveling singers to magic shows. Other than circuses, touring opera house performers provided the only professional entertainment available in small towns and their performances were well attended.

Parades were probably the most exciting organized activity to extend the length of main street. They were sponsored by many different groups and included many participants. Livestock

Fig. 69

Parades were frequent events along small-town main streets. They were organized by many groups, ranging from veteran, service and fraternal organizations to Sunday school teachers, temperance advocates and circuses. Towns with resident Chinese, such as Huntington, even celebrated the Chinese New Year with parades. Drawing both marchers and watchers to main street, these rituals accentuated its social role. At the turn of the century, one of a town's most important events was its Fourth of July parade; this at Elgin in 1899. (Courtesy Ethel Chandler, Elgin)

show, county fair and circus parades proceeded regularly down main streets. In addition, parades were held by Red Cross chapters, fraternal organizations, women's auxiliaries, even Sunday school teachers. The Fourth of July (see **fig. 69**) parade was always the year's most elaborate, with street decorations, bands, floats, decorated wagons and buggies, and marching units. The fraternal lodge parades, on the other hand, were simple affairs with perhaps a band to accompany the lodge members as they marched in uniform down the street. Parades attached a ritual importance to the main street. Their frequency and varied nature meant that everyone in the town likely had a chance to march in one, enhancing each person's sense of involvement

151

with the social institution of main street, and, by extension, with the community.

The casual social activities that took place along main streets may have been less spectacular than the organized events but they were not less important. Some occurred at particular times and places while others developed out of chance encounters. The stage stop (usually in front of the hotel), and, later, the railroad depot were popular gathering places. In Elgin, the typical Sunday included church services, Sunday dinner and an afternoon stroll up main street to the depot, to greet the train. Rowdier weekday socializing transpired in the saloons and billiard halls located along the streets.

Along the streets and in the stores, casual encounters were common. Most town residents walked to main street, increasing the likelihood of seeing friends and stopping for a chat. The social importance of this excursion is indicated by the fact that ladies "dressed" when they went shopping.

Main streets were social centers, officially important places where significant things happened. The activities they hosted were traditions, being part of the town's established order. Organized community events occurred along main street, which also provided the setting for a rich collection of informal gatherings and interactions, in their own way regular and ordered. Clearly, main street played an important role in individuals' lives, as well as contributing to the well being of the town. Much of the sentiment that bound a town together, instilling its members with a sense of community, was rooted in the social activities that took place along main street.

Summary

Most main streets started out in much the same fashion. Their initial construction was financed by imported capital that came in with the influx of new businessmen. The street, which had an open appearance, encompassed a wide variety of services and activities. The earliest entrepreneurs generally stayed only a short time, for in most cases the business district was overbuilt and the hinterland population proved insufficient to support all of the town's merchants and tradesmen. But those who left were quickly replaced by others and so, despite the generally discouraging returns, main street business communities continued to grow. Most stage 2 and stage 3 main streets developed according to this pattern, built by expanding but unstable business communities. As the surrounding areas were settled more densely and patronage increased, they began to prosper.

Stage 4 main streets developed as the result of a new phenomenon in the towns' business communities: a stable core of long-term members. They generally owned the town's biggest businesses and were supported by a large hinterland population. Unlike their predecessors they prospered. These persistent businessmen used locally generated profits to replace the pioneer main street buildings with others more characteristic of larger towns. These merchants came to dominate the street, their establishments joined by increasing numbers of specialized businesses.

It should be noted that certain towns did not follow the development sequence described above. These were the mining and railroad-construction towns, with comparatively narrow economic bases and distinctive resident and transient population groups. These groups arrived quickly in large numbers, requiring and frequenting distinctive types of businesses, which lined the hastily built, high-density main streets.

Later
Main Street
Developments

VI

THE EVOLUTION of main streets in northeastern Oregon since about 1925 has been in marked contrast to that which went before. Up to 1925, main streets were being built; after that year, construction generally stopped and dismantling began. By the mid-1930s, many of northeastern Oregon's main street businesses had closed and their buildings stood empty. The economic and social roles of many of the region's main streets were drastically reduced.

Nonetheless, the importance of main streets to the small towns of northeastern Oregon persists. Their economic and social roles have been maintained, modifications notwithstanding. Some have lost a large part of their economic function but the social role continues to draw people to them. Some towns, too, have recently experienced population growth. This is reflected by new construction and other improvements along the main streets. In these towns, a new cycle of development has begun.

Decline

"Decline" usually refers to decline in the prosperity of main street business districts rather than to the less marked decrease in main street social activities. Small-town main streets declined for a number of reasons. As previously explained, some declined soon after founding because an adequate economic base never developed. Others declined less immediately. The two determining factors in this slower decline were depopulation and increased mobility. Diminishing rural and town populations reduced local business; at the same time, the arrival of automobiles increased mobility, and it became convenient for shoppers to

155

Fig. 70

Main street, Cornucopia, about 1925. When this photograph was taken Cornucopia was nearly 40 years old and already beginning to appear quaint. The decline of the town is clear; had it been prospering in the 1920s it would have resembled other towns of its age—the false-front and wooden balconied buildings would have been replaced by structures of brick, main street would have been paved and continuous pedestrian walkways constructed. (OHS neg. 47394)

travel to larger towns whose main streets offered a wider selection of goods at lower prices.

Decline in main street prosperity is certainly noticeable but difficult to document. The number of people in business along the street has already been discussed as one index of prosperity, and the number of buildings along it has been proposed as another. A comparison of the rates of construction and destruction is also revealing. Sanborn maps and tax records help to identify the point at which the rate of main street building destruction begins to exceed the rate of construction. Consecutive Sanborn coverage of a single main street documents building longevity and rate of replacement. Tax records do the same for more recent years (the health of a main street is reflected by the value of its land and buildings, and tax assessments graph the rise and fall of main street property values).

Building Longevity and Replacement

Continuing construction along main street indicates continued prosperity. A prospering business community encourages, and often requires, main street expansion. Conversely, a decline in prosperity and size of the business community results in building abandonment and removal.

Several towns in northeastern Oregon were mapped at regular intervals by the Sanborn Map Company, making it possible to follow the initial construction, replacement and removal of their main street buildings. Among these, Summerville is the most complete case study. Its decline began shortly after Sanborn coverage commenced; maps of the town were published in 1888, 1890, 1900 and 1910.

Figure 71 graphs the persistence of individual buildings along Summerville's main street. In 1888, the town's businesses were just beginning to feel Elgin's competition. A fire at that time burned much of the western side of the street, but it was rebuilt by 1890. Buildings destroyed after 1890, however, were not necessarily replaced, and by 1910 the west side of the street contained only half as many buildings as in 1888. Though the town's main street had declined by 1910, it continued to function as a business district during the decade. The final commercial collapse of the street, and the removal of its buildings, came after 1910. In 1975, a little more than a century after Summerville's platting, only three buildings stood along the west side of the street, of which only one was an operating commercial establishment; the others were an 1874 lodge hall and a 1905 house.

Comparison of figure 72 with figure 71 indicates that the decline in the number of buildings along Summerville's main street closely parallels the decline in the size of the business community. Although difficult to document in all cases, it is likely that this relationship applies in other towns as well. Unfortunately, Sanborn coverage of most small towns stopped around 1910, by which time decline had not generally set in. In a few cases mapping continued until 1930, after which time all small-town cov-

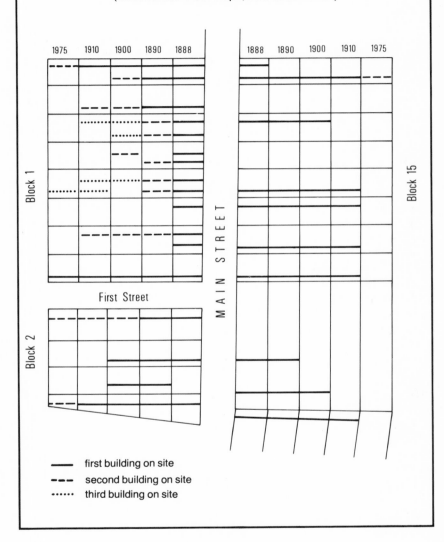

BUILDING LONGEVITY & REPLACEMENT
SUMMERVILLE
(from Sanborn Co. maps, field observation)

Fig. 71

1975　1910　1900　1890　1888　　1888　1890　1900　1910　1975

Block 1

Block 2

Block 15

MAIN STREET

First Street

——— first building on site
- - - second building on site
······ third building on site

158

erage in northeastern Oregon ceased. Detailed business directory coverage of small towns also stopped in the 1930s as their commercial importance in the region waned. An examination of more recent decline, therefore, must incorporate other sources.

Property Value Trends

The value of individual lots and buildings along a street reflects a business district's general condition. Tax records provide these hard facts and so, together with information about the nature of standing buildings and those that preceded them, can be used to determine when a street's decline began.

The tax assessor assigns two values to a property: the value of the land and the value of improvements on it. The former reflects the basic land value while the latter indicates the relative condition and quality of the buildings on the property. Since such information is helpful in reconstructing a picture of main street, it is unfortunate that tax figures are generally difficult to retrieve. Changes in ownership, division of property and changes in both assessing policies and record-keeping practices, complicate following the history of a single property's value.

Two of the northeastern Oregon towns that saw their main street decline were Summerville and North Powder. The appraised land value of the lots in these two towns changed insignificantly between the early 1900s and the 1970s. Land values in Summerville rose gradually, but in North Powder they peaked in the late 1920s and then declined. The average main street lot in North Powder in the early 1900s was worth about four times that of one in Summerville, probably because of its superior location with respect to highway and railroad. The average lot increased in value as the town grew, but after North Powder lost its principal industry (ice production for refrigerated rail cars), the town declined and so did its property values.

The changes in the value of property improvements along Summerville's and North Powder's main streets are more striking. These changes document the deterioration of buildings along the streets and their eventual removal. (The appraised value of a building reflects its quality, condition and potential

159

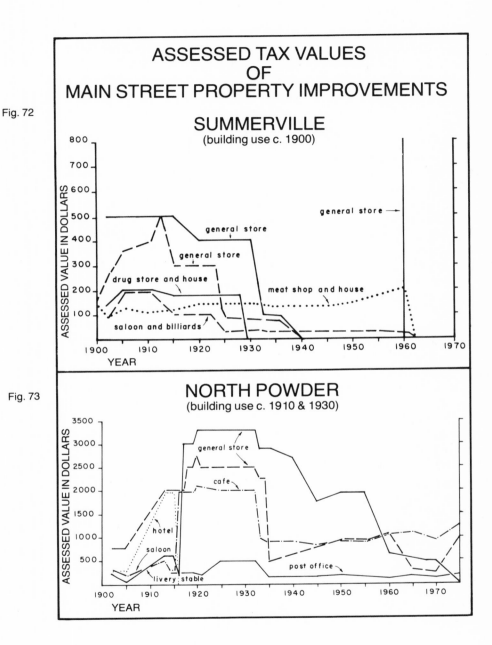

Fig. 72

ASSESSED TAX VALUES
OF
MAIN STREET PROPERTY IMPROVEMENTS

SUMMERVILLE
(building use c. 1900)

Fig. 73

NORTH POWDER
(building use c. 1910 & 1930)

160

use. Once a building is abandoned, its condition deteriorates and its value drops.)

Figures 72 and 73 trace the assessed property improvement values of selected lots in Summerville and North Powder from 1902 to 1970. The lots were selected for their relatively complete tax records. Each property is identified on the diagrams as to its use in 1900 (Summerville) or 1910 (North Powder), as indicated on Sanborn maps and old photographs.

The lots in Summerville are those in main street blocks 1 and 15, previously used as examples of early main street development and decline (see **figs. 43, 45** and **71**). The peak of Summerville's prosperity was long past by 1910, the date of the last Sanborn map. The blocks' last buildings were removed in the 1930s and by 1940 only two of the five lots studied still had buildings on them (the third "property improvement" consisted of a fence). However, in 1960 a new building was erected on Lot 1, which currently houses the Summerville Store (and post office, gas station and tavern), the last retail establishment left on the street.

North Powder's prosperity continued through the 1920s. In this town, which developed a stage 3 main street, the distinction between what were wood buildings and those that had been brick or stone is revealed by the formers' lower appraisals. A fire in 1915 burned most of main street, leaving only the brick and stone buildings. New structures were erected on some of the lots and their values soared. The assessed values crested during the period of maximum population in North Powder. Diminution of population was accompanied by a reduction in the value of both the land and the improvements along the street. The general economic depression of the 1930s served to accelerate the decline of North Powder's main street.

Summerville and North Powder are only two of a number of towns in northeastern Oregon that have experienced main street decline. Yet several observations hold true for all of them.

The first refers to the earlier discussion about stages of main street development. Tax data show that beyond the physical changes of building density and construction materials, progress through the stages was reflected in increased land values. Buildings also tended to be worth more as the town developed. In-

161

terestingly, in both Summerville and North Powder hotel and general store buildings had the highest appraised values.

A second generalization concerns the time lag between business decline and decline in property values. After the first buildings along a main street were removed without being replaced, the rest of the street followed suit. The period of this time lag was not set, but generally within 15 years the property values along most of the main street became seriously depressed and many buildings were removed.

While land values in small towns have increased modestly, the value of property improvements has substantially declined. Many buildings have been razed and those that remain are worth only a fraction of their former value. Tax data trends indicate the continuation or cessation of main street's economic support. With additional information about building longevity and replacement rates, it is possible to date and measure main street decline.

Building Removal: Its Effect on Main Street

Buildings were cleared from main street both intentionally and as a result of accident. Nearly every main street in northeastern Oregon has lost buildings to fire. Often clearing town blocks, accidental fires could be an effective renewal agent—if the town's economic base was sufficiently strong to support reconstruction, the destroyed buildings and streets were soon rebuilt. However, burned-out buildings and blocks in less prosperous towns were not always rebuilt. This was often the case for mining towns, which, with a large number of closely placed wood buildings that burned quickly, were most completely devastated by fire. Their prosperity was so transitory that their main streets flourished only briefly. If these streets burned during the period of decline, they were never rebuilt. The August, 1917 fire in Sumpter burned the entire downtown; figure 74 shows its appearance in 1976 (from the north end of the main street, looking southward along its length).

Deliberate demolition of main street buildings was a second removal process which, with the development of better fire-fighting equipment and techniques, was more frequently imple-

162

Fig. 74

Sumpter's main street, 1976, looking south. This snowy street is the entire length of Sumpter's former main street, the buildings along which
burned in 1917. Mining activity had subsided by that time, and the business community did not rebuild. A few broken bricks and slight depres-
sions from former basements are all that remain to indicate the main
street. (B. R. Bailey)

mented. Building removal was a necessary part of main street
development as it made space for newer, larger buildings. Inten-
tional removal without replacement, however, was part of the
process of decline (and was not widely practiced until the 1960s).
Reduction in business community size resulted in a number of
vacated buildings. After many years of vacancy, buildings
deemed unsafe and uneconomical to repair were removed. In
some towns, the net effect of this has been almost as great as a
destructive fire. Along Huntington's main street, for example,
nearly all of the wood buildings have now been removed, leaving
isolated brick and stone buildings.

Accidental fire and deliberate demolition combined can elimi-
nate most of the structures along a town's main street. Figures 75
and 76 compare North Powder's main street in 1911 and 1975.

163

Fig. 75

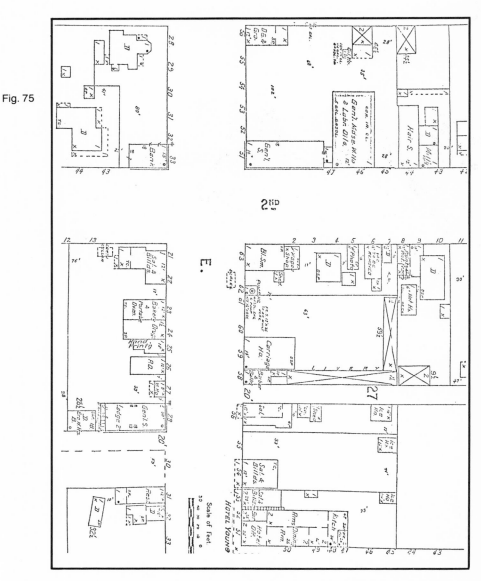

Main street, North Powder, 1911. At this time North Powder had a well
developed stage 2 main street. After a fire in 1916, it was rebuilt as a stage
3 street. (Courtesy Sanborn Map Co., Inc.)

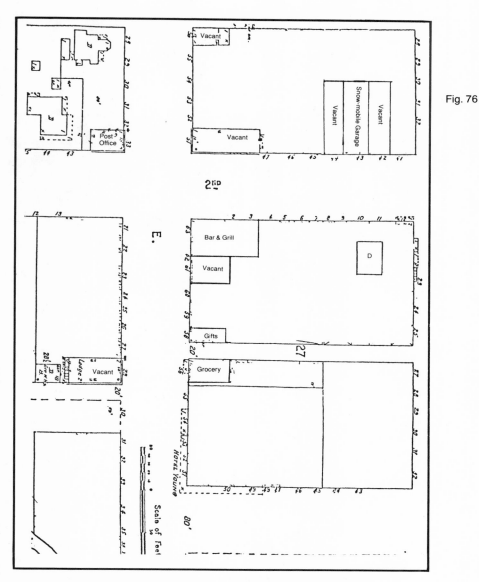

Fig. 76

Main street, North Powder, 1975. Economic decline in the 1930s resulted in building abandonment and eventual destruction. (Map base courtesy Sanborn Map Co., Inc.)

Fig. 77

Main street, North Powder, about 1929. This stage 3 street is almost solidly lined by grocery shops, dry goods establishments and cigar stores, cafes and other businesses. Nearly all were housed in brick and stone buildings. (OHS neg. 16877)

Many of the 1911 buildings were destroyed in the 1916 fire, but the street was rebuilt as a stage 3 main street. Business failure in the 1930s caused abandonment of many buildings and, ultimately, their demolition. This effected a shift from the stage 3 street seen in figure 77 down to the stage 2 street in figure 78.

The cycle of building, burning, building and demolition experienced by North Powder's main street is one of the more extreme examples of construction and destruction in northeastern Oregon. However, each of the region's main streets has undergone some aspects of the cycle, and in recent years more buildings have been torn down than built along most of them. The removal of buildings and the reduced intensity of use has resulted in a shift of main streets to a building pattern typical of their earlier years. Most of them (but not all) have in effect reverted to an earlier stage of development.

166

Main street, North Powder, 1976. Some of the street's original buildings are now missing, others stand vacant. However, a constant stream of people coming in on business and for leisurely visits with others still fill the grocery, the post office, and the two-story Powder Club. (B. R. Bailey)

Main Streets Today

Economic Change and Main Street Adjustments

The economy of northeastern Oregon has undergone a number of major changes since the era of town founding. Some once-important elements of the economy have declined or disappeared altogether while others have grown and new ones have emerged. Mining and railroading have both declined and the towns that depended on them have experienced the greatest retrenchment. Rural farm populations have diminished and the rural service centers without supplementary income sources have declined as well. New elements of the regional economy include tourism and the lumber industry. Summer tourists and hunters in the fall have bolstered business along some of the

Wallowa, 1962. Although the lumber industry has been an important factor in the economy of northeastern Oregon towns, the industry itself is unstable and in many communities main street prosperity has fluctuated as a result. In 1962, a strike by the 235-member lumber and sawmill workers local 2966 in Wallowa caused the town's merchants a great deal of worry about the future of their businesses. (OHS, *Oregon Journal* Coll.)

main streets that formerly primarily depended on a rural hinterland population. The towns that have declined the least are those with an economic base associated with the lumber industry. Logging long has been a part of the regional economy but large operations have been consolidated in the larger towns within the last 30 years. The industry itself, however, is unstable and the prosperity of the larger towns' main streets has fluctuated as a result.

Stage 2 streets have adjusted to the decline in their surrounding rural population. Although their business communities have been reduced, as have the numbers of buildings along the main streets, the towns have not entirely lost their economic role. Groceries (some with gas pumps out front), post offices, taverns and cafes still exist along their main streets. Town populations have not declined as much as might be expected. The same mobility that reduced the business along the main streets has also made it possible for town residents to commute to jobs elsewhere. Town populations are still large enough to support some businesses. Lostine and Imbler are two examples of rural service centers that have become bedroom communities, retaining their main streets and sense of identity.

168

Fig. 79

The stage 2 main streets are also those that have most benefited by the development of the tourist industry. Towns that once
drew miners now draw tourists as ghost towns. Cornucopia,
Sumpter and other nearby ghost towns in the Blues are favor-
ites. The construction of dams has also created two lakes on the
Snake River and one on the Powder; these draw many tourists.
The economy of Halfway, once stimulated by mining and railroad construction, is now stimulated by the visitors who come for
different reasons. Richland has become a supply depot for boat-
ers and hunters, who supplement the town's income from its
diminished rural farm population. Today, almost all of the old
main street buildings in Lostine, Imbler, Halfway and Richland
are occupied.

Stage 3 and stage 4 towns developed because they had rail
connections and some form of industry. They declined if their
importance in rail operations was reduced or if their local industry shut down. Huntington and North Powder are two prime
examples of towns adversely affected by railroad decisions or
loss of a local industry. The economies of Union, Elgin, Wallowa
(**fig. 79**) and Joseph all have been based on the lumber industry
for many years. Their surrounding rural populations all have

Robinette depot on the road, 1958. Although a lake created by dam construction on the Powder River draws an increasing number of tourists to the area, the Brownlee Reservoir also inundated the Baker County towns of Copperfield (founded in 1907) and Robinette (founded in 1908) as well as a 37-mile railroad branch line. Here, the Robinette depot is on its way to Pine Valley for conversion into a church building. (OHS, *Oregon Journal* Coll.)

declined and the maintenance of their main street has depended increasingly on the lumber industry. However, the closing of a sawmill easily can result in the loss of a quarter of a town's population. Main street decline resulting from rural depopulation has been averted but main street stability is not guaranteed. There is little new construction along these streets, but, on the other hand, they are still fairly complete. Few buildings are missing and there is a wide variety of stores.

Social Life Along Main Streets Today

The social functions along main streets continue to constitute an important unifying element of town life. Organized activities have become less significant, but informal associations are maintained and constantly renewed. The social role of the main street has continued to draw people to this central area even in towns whose business communties have failed.

At one time, all small towns had at least one fraternal organization which met in a main street lodge hall. Population decline and alternative forms of entertainment have caused fraternal organization membership to drop. Today, many chapters and lodges have become inactive and those still active meet less frequently.

Parades, another organized form of main street activity, also occur less frequently. The larger towns continue to hold parades, but Fourth-of-July parades, circus parades and fraternal organization parades are a thing of the past. Those of today are likely to be associated with other town activites such as fairs, livestock shows or rodeos. These parades are still major activities, however, drawing many of their participants from other towns, and they are well attended. The parades, widely advertised, now serve to promote and maintain town identity. They reinforce the social role of main street and strengthen the individual participants' sense of involvement with the town.

Informal social activities occur regularly. They are centered in cafes and taverns, found on every main street. These establishments are patronized by different groups in the course of the day. That cafes have emerged as the busiest businesses in small towns is indicated by the fact that they are often in the newest buildings on main street.

Figure 81 illustrates the daily main street social cycle in Union; here, various main street sites become centers of activity at certain times. The most concentrated activity occurs when school lets out. Union's schools are situated along the southern end of main street and many students walk and drive up the street on their way home. Those who cruise the street in automobiles create their own parade. In cruising main street, young people are acknowledging its central status and establishing a relationship with it, which could prove beneficial to main street businesses.

The importance of main street as a social center is most apparent in the towns that have suffered the greatest economic decline. Other businesses may close but the cafes and taverns re-

171

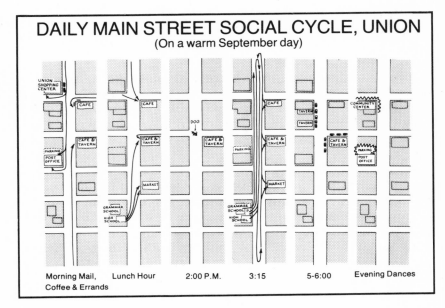

DAILY MAIN STREET SOCIAL CYCLE, UNION
(On a warm September day)

Fig. 81

| Morning Mail, Coffee & Errands | Lunch Hour | 2:00 P.M. | 3:15 | 5-6:00 | Evening Dances |

main open. In Durkee, the cafe is the only establishment left on main street—and it rocks with country and western music from the jukebox as the town residents gather for a mid-morning cup of coffee. North Powder's main street is quiet during the day but the Powder Club, a bar-and-grill, blazes with lights on Friday nights, the street around it filled with cars. People may go to a larger town to shop but when they want to see their friends, they go to their own main street.

Problems and Challenges for the Future

Main streets today have adjusted to the changes that began in the 1920s and 1930s: rural depopulation, loss of local industry and increased competition from other towns resulting from greater accessibility by automobile. The size of their business communities has decreased and the permanently vacant buildings have been removed. Recently, hinterland populations have begun to stabilize and many of the region's towns actually have experienced a population increase between 1970 and 1980. The stage may be set for a new cycle of main street construction.

Problems

The basic problem facing most main streets today is that future town construction is not likely to occur along them. Main streets today face competition from within their own towns. Other locations seem increasingly attractive as sites for new business buildings. Two recent phenomena are threatening main streets today, both related to the automobile. The first is the change in shopping patterns. The second is interstate highway construction.

Main street building patterns evolved prior to the arrival of the automobile. Main street business districts were traversed only by pedestrians; local patrons walked from home to main street, and out-of-town visitors, arriving by horse and wagon, left their vehicle on a side street or at the livery stable. Thus, main streets essentially resembled modern shopping centers: designed for pedestrian traffic, densely lined by businesses and providing "off-street parking." Shoppers assumed that they would walk the length of main street, just as today's shoppers enter malls knowing they have some walking ahead of them.

The majority of today's small-town main street customers drive to main street, intending to park as closely as possible to their place of business. Business proprietors attempt to facilitate this by seeking locations with superior access and parking facilities. Such sites are seldom found along main street. Consequently, building construction scatters, spreading to the margins of the main street and elsewhere.

For northeastern Oregon's towns, the greatest danger of dispersed construction is that the main streets may ultimately be vacated, creating an impression of decline and failure not necessarily indicative of the town's true business climate. Credit and loans for new main street construction could then become more difficult to secure and remaining businessmen along the street

Fig. 82

Huntington, 1978. Huntington's main street is now quiet compared to its turn-of-the-century appearance, but the size and style of the remaining buildings indicate the town's former importance. All of the buildings in view here are empty, except the one associated with the gas station and two small structures with cars parked in front. The latter two are important socializing centers: the post office (with the low white roof) and a tavern next door (with its original saloon furnishings). On a vacant lot where a bank once stood sits a small grandstand (it had been set up for a Fourth of July dance on main street). (B. R. Bailey)

might find themselves stranded. Premature judgement of failure can effectively bring on the condition. This may have happened to the main street of Huntington (**fig. 82**), which has been virtually abandoned, although nearly 500 people live there. Opportunity exists in Huntington, but financing of a new business may be difficult to obtain because of the atmosphere of decline.

Highway traffic has always been an important element in main street business. Towns were platted along roads, or if that was impossible, the road was rerouted to pass through town. The towns along the Oregon Trail in particular prospered as traffic increased. The construction of an interstate highway past these

174

Fig. 83

The Imbler Cafe (left foreground), 1976, does a good business and plays an important part in community socializing. Other businesses along this typical northeastern Oregon stage 2 main street serving one of the region's rural areas include a small market with gas pumps, a farm equipment repair garage, and a blacksmith shop. The former livery stable still stands, but is unused. The two-story brick building on the right was built as a general store with lodgings on the second floor. The ground floor now holds the post office and a second-hand store; lodgings are still rented. (B. R. Bailey)

towns, and various highway realignments affecting others, has removed important economic support by diverting traffic from main streets. Traffic and main street were synonymous for nearly a century in the region and separation of the two has proved deleterious.

Town businessmen have responded to the loss of highway traffic by attempting to reunite the highway and business district. The process is well illustrated in North Powder. The town's main street conveys an impression of failure. However, a new grocery store, cafe and gas station are located west of main street, closer to the interstate highway. If these establishments

Fig. 84

Union's main street, 1976. Union has the oldest stage 4 main street in northeastern Oregon. The town grew as Union County's seat and its growth ceased when it lost that function to La Grande. The city hall (at left) was built in 1891, the two-story masonic lodge (down the street) shortly thereafter. The Baptist Church on the corner was originally a general store. Recent main street construction has produced smaller-scale buildings such as the laundry at the center. (B. R. Bailey)

were located instead on main street, North Powder's former business district would have a very different appearance.

The buildings that are constructed along main streets today are of a different scale from that of their predecessors—they are smaller and plainer. The scale difference is least evident along stage 2 main streets, with their tradition of open space and smaller buildings. The new Imbler Cafe, shown in figure 83, corresponds to the rest of that town's main street in scale, but the laundry in figure 84 is clearly not in keeping with Union's stage 4 main street buildings.

Essentially, main streets are regressing to earlier stages of development. Building size and density have decreased, while

Fig. 85

Main street, Enterprise, about 1924. Enterprise, the county seat of Wallowa County, had a fully developed stage 4 main street. Most of its buildings were brick or stone, and most were two stories high. (This photograph was taken in the opposite direction from the view shown in fig. 55.) (OHS neg. 63368)

open areas have increased, even on main streets with prosperous business communities and growing populations. Frequently, facade modifications disguise the older buildings and remove much of their decorative contribution to the street. Figures 85 and 86, photographs of the principal main street blocks in Enterprise, illustrate the kinds of changes occurring on stage 4 main streets throughout the region.

Challenges

The greatest challenge facing main streets today is the challenge to retain their cohesion. Aging buildings need repair or replacement. Too often, neither is done; rather, new structures are built elsewhere. However, some of northeastern Oregon's

Fig. 86

main streets are being maintained in modified form through recent construction. The new buildings are generally smaller than those of the past; nevertheless, their location on main street contributes to the longevity of the business district.

Small towns can expect to grow in the future. Nationwide statistics indicate that migration to larger cities is slowing and that growth is now occurring in the smaller cities and towns. The trend is already evident in some of the small towns of northeastern Oregon. Planned and built for larger populations than they now have, the small towns of the region should be able to absorb this growth easily. While larger towns and cities contemplate the expense and inconvenience of growth, the towns of northeastern Oregon already have the essential facilities and services: schools, police and fire departments, streets and sidewalks, streetlights and street maintenance equipment. Many of the towns are now planning improved water and sewage systems. Increased population within the towns will be welcomed and readily accommodated.

Main street, Enterprise, 1976. Only the ground floors of main street buildings are still in use. Note that the Mansard roof has been removed from the hotel in the distance. The old Wallowa National Bank building (foreground) has been reduced to one story. (B. R. Bailey)

Thus, it is essential that northeastern Oregon's small towns realize the significance of their main streets. Like early main street builders, today's business investors must realize that the success of a town depends to some extent on how busy the main street appears and that their close association will help to heighten an atmosphere of activity.

The attraction of people to main street has always been a basic fact of life in northeastern Oregon's small towns and has resulted in social patterns that accentuate the street's importance. This attraction has persisted even in towns with relatively empty main streets. It indicates that main streets are still a vital part of this region's small towns and that, given proper attention, the streets and towns have potential for significant future development.

179

TABLE 1
BAKER COUNTY POPULATION, 1870-1980

	1870	1880	1890	1900
BAKER DIVISION				
Baker, all precincts and city	312	1258	2519	6933
Depot			524	69
South Baker				506
	312	1258	3043	7508
BAKER VALLEY DIVISION				
Alder			159	283
Virtue		156		317
Baker Country				
Stewart				
	0	156	159	600
EAGLE VALLEY DIVISION				
Eagle Creek	160			
Eagle Valley (lower Eagle)		223	349	766
Precinct 1				
Precinct 2				
Sparta (Eagle)		235	146	171
Bed Rock		98	134	144
Sanger			93	12
East Eagle				38
Daley			17	
Copper Butte				103
Big Creek				
Lookout				
Robinette				
	160	556	739	1234
HALFWAY DIVISION				
Cornucopia			182	359
Iron Dyke				193
Pine			621	930
Precinct 1				
Precinct 2				
Copperfield				
	0	0	803	1481

Note: Names in parentheses are former names of precincts.

1910	1920	1930	1940	1950	1960	1970	1980
4617	6268	7858	9342	9471			
2086	1224						
933	943						
7636	8435	7858	9342	9471	9986	9354	10418
288	274	215	147	108			
164	57	25					
		691	384	412			
			162	157			
452	331	931	693	677	744	725	
108							
	670	823	815	675			
	593	251	222	201			
123	249	141	135	53			
267	207	388	276	271			
18							
86	73						
189	212	163	179	140			
	68	45	24				
	113	75	69	38			
1791	2185	1886	1720	1378	1219	829	995
132	242	11	477				
949	251	193	105	58			
674	897	904	867	657			
700	594	509	528	448			
	207						
2455	2191	1617	1977	1163	2368	1148	1536

(continued)

Table 1, (continued)

	1870	1880	1890	1900
HEREFORD DIVISION				
Auburn	442	202	189	
Bridgeport (Clark's Ck.)	342	187	282	17?
Sumpter		261	91	185
Hereford (Clearyville, Cleary)	61	208	279	17?
Cracker			83	
Clifford (Parker)			69	53
Unity				25?
Greenhorn				
McEwen				29?
Bourne				59?
Columbia				
Audrey				
Britten			192	
	784	711	1114	398
HUNTINGTON DIVISION				
Conner Creek		145	136	15
Huntington (Burnt R.)	79	218	417	10?
Rye Valley	73	122	120	14
Durkee (Express)			418	4?
Weatherby				14
	152	485	1091	18?
WINGVILLE DIVISION				
Powder River Valley	783			
North Powder		276	115	1?
Pocahontas		542	366	3?
Wingville		187	252	1?
Haines			261	3?
Rock Creek			33	4?
Elkhorn (Willow)			67	1?
Muddy			246	
	783	1005	1340	16?
COUNTY TOTAL	2191	4171	8289	183?

182

910	1920	1930	1940	1950	1960	1970	1980
96	75	106	115	61			
584	233	188	461	168			
137	154	191	236				
123	246	71	31				
308	254	241	291	284			
59	45	22	8				
202	218	205	160	54			
220							
	39						
	45	47	80				
868	1292	1034	1337	803	714	716	875
97	102	91	123	76			
997	931	1082	974	937			
54	72	81	50	37			
21	388	328	291	210			
73	94	85	73	60			
42	1587	1667	1511	1320	1112	758	729
33	240	279	188	136			
96	300	194	285	233			
61	804	760	763	670			
28	564	528	481	324			
14							
32	1908	1761	1717	1363	1152	1326	1581
76	17929	16754	18297	16175	17295	14919	16134

rce: U.S. Census of Population, 1860-1970; *Census Advance Reports*, 1980.

183

TABLE 2
UNION COUNTY POPULATION, 1870-1980

	1870	1880	1890	190
COVE DIVISION				
Cove	583	631	801	87
Alicel				56
Imbler				
	583	631	801	143
ELGIN DIVISION				
Summerville	320	800	1275	122
Elgin (Indian Valley)		563	1332	208
Palmer				
	320	1363	2607	33
GRANDE RONDE DIVISION				
Grande Ronde	119	65		
La Grande	640	836	481	124
Island (Iowa)	320	735	682	74
Perry				3
	1079	1636	1163	234
LA GRANDE DIVISION				
La Grande City			2583	299
	0	0	2583	299
STARKEY DIVISION				
Camp Carson			34	4
Starkey			130	1
Hilgard			988	64
Kamela				
	0	0	1152	8
UNION DIVISION				
Union	400	979	1219	160
Big Creek		159	265	20
Powder		200	599	49
Antelope			130	
Hot Lake				
	400	1338	2213	24
COUNTY TOTAL	2392	4968	10519	133

Note: Names in parentheses are former names of precincts.

910	1920	1930	1940	1950	1960	1970	1980
100	980	815	746	781			
364	297	346	274	278			
410	452	452	388	322			
374	1729	1613	1408	1381	1270	1350	1801
784	501	477	454	452			
466	1815	1467	1756	1955			
	122						
250	2438	1944	2210	2407	2391	2566	3441
166	1140	1685	1712	1768			
760	373	330	384	368			
266	272	145	104	129			
192	1785	2160	2200	2265	2590	2896	
343	6913	8050	7747	8635	9014	9645	
343	6913	8050	7747	8635	9014	9645	15314
8			13	2			
70	63	107	182	169			
17	127	182	93	86			
99	90	114	60				
94	280	403	348	257	216	355	121
47	1732	1610	1872	1697			
27	140	302	542	425			
68	1026	963	738	612			
96	280	133	108	94			
	313	314	226	189			
38	3491	3322	3486	3017	2699	2565	3244
91	16636	17492	17399	17962	18180	19377	23921

rce: U.S. Census of Population, 1860, 1970; Census Advance Reports, 1980.

TABLE 3
WALLOWA COUNTY POPULATION, 1890-1980

	1890	1900	1910
FLORA DIVISION			
Paradise	177	579	273
Lost Prairie	133	269	188
Grouse		179	308
Flora			320
Mud Creek			94
	310	1027	1183
IMNAHA DIVISION			
Three Buck	151		
Park		117	161
Imnaha	83	182	216
Pittsburg			45
Pine Creek	169	200	161
Butte			95
OK Gulch			
Enterprise Precinct 3 (excluding city)			
	403	499	678
JOSEPH			
Joseph	668	572	1196
Prairie Creek	280	359	367
Divide		42	118
	948	973	1681
ENTERPRISE			
Enterprise	617	865	1703
Trout Creek (Swamp Creek)	233	297	230
Enterprise precincts 1, 2, 4			
Enterprise Precinct 3 city population			
	850	1162	1933
WALLOWA DIVISION			
Lostine	530	686	615
Wallowa	620	1010	1629
Promise		181	308
Powwatka			85
Leap			252
Evans			
Smith Mountain			
Maxville			
	1150	1877	2889
COUNTY TOTAL	3661	5538	8364

Note: Names in parentheses are former names of precincts.

186

1920	1930	1940	1950	1960	1970	1980
300	147					
147	114					
287	171	215	252			
328	208	453	275			
83	53					
1145	693	668	527	291	217	213
107	103	83	60			
193	142	195	139			
59	61					
253	135	88				
111	293	151				
72						
			209			
795	734	517	408	316	250	245
1323	1001	1345	1532			
342	272					
77	124	146				
1742	1397	1491	1532	1501	1446	1745
2547	2287	2501				
224						
			2007			
			292			
2771	2287	2501	2299	2763	2513	3189
398	314	590	579			
1672	1501	1572	1846			
245	161	177	73			
79	75	45				
207						
266	318					
458	131	62				
	203					
3325	2703	2446	2498	2231	1821	1881
9778	7814	7623	7264	7102	6247	7273

rce: U.S. Census of Population, 1880-1970; Census Advance Reports, 1980.

TABLE 4
FARM TRENDS

	Number of All Farms	% Land Area in Farms	Small Grains* (Acres)
BAKER COUNTY			
1900	725		12,655
1910	1,305	15.2	23,850
1920	1,509	25.0	30,360
1930	1,383	34.1	29,327
1940	1,259	40.3	21,125
1950	1,052	46.8	35,123
1960	757	45.2	27,103
1970	626	40.7	13,594
1978	627	47.9	16,689
UNION COUNTY			
1900	1,481		58,181
1910	1,309	29.6	67,376
1920	1,279	34.4	69,053
1930	1,276	35.7	70,825
1940	1,255	36.2	52,217
1950	1,092	39.7	61,588
1960	873	40.6	57,085
1970	678	37.2	57,429
1978	655	36.0	53,679
WALLOWA COUNTY			
1900	803		13,759
1910	1,058	17.6	22,460
1920	1,149	25.8	42,626
1930	952	28.1	46,978
1940	989	28.5	30,834
1950	780	33.5	38,057
1960	600	35.8	31,375
1970	423	33.1	29,266
1978	444	38.4	42,162

*Including wheat
†Including dairy cattle

Wheat (Acres)	Sheep	Dairy Cattle	All Cattle†
	140,759	2,951	29,610
8,490	149,933	4,802	14,679
9,885	104,255	8,820	48,528
7,445	177,084	10,571	44,095
0,097	59,229	9,462	41,342
21,837	61,052	5,706	64,856
5,343	28,133	1,237	85,937
7,964	16,976	2,669	88,435
7,614	5,773	1,649	106,207
	65,020	5,079	21,339
1,487	24,229	4,681	4,048
5,749	19,580	7,684	14,383
8,750	67,653	5,571	19,050
36,038	17,515	7,225	15,590
9,742	4,404	3,878	23,793
7,171	7,163	2,108	33,993
7,559	4,481	579	34,268
7,655	3,315	400	41,224
	46,830	2,242	14,233
2,265	224,161	3,426	8,463
33,204	87,782	6,182	36,050
35,629	124,109	4,603	23,620
19,325	64,954	7,294	25,877
27,393	24,522	4,408	38,088
18,784	19,076	1,782	43,725
19,651	21,316	495	52,000
21,423	12,809	291	60,022

Source: U.S. Census of Agriculture, 1900-1978

189

TABLE 5
PIONEER TOWNS FOUNDED 1860-1889

NAME	PLAT DATE	ECONOMIC BASE‡	STILL A TOWN IN 1980?
Auburn (B)*	1862 (P.O.)†	Mining	No
Bridgeport (B)	1862 (P.O.)	Mining	No
Clarksville (B)	1862 (P.O.)	Mining	No
Baker (B)	1864	Road	Yes
Union (U)	1864	Road	Yes
La Grande (U)	1868	Road	Yes
Oro Dell (U)	1868	Road	No
Sparta (B)	1872 (P.O.)	Mining	No
Summerville (U)	1873	Road	Yes
Cove (U)	1874	Road	Yes
Island City (U)	1874	Road	Yes
Joseph (W)	1883	R.S.C.	Yes
Lostine (W)	1884	R.S.C.	Yes
Telocaset (U)	1885 (P.O.)	Railroad	No
North Powder (U)	1885	Railroad	Yes
Elgin (U)	1886	Railroad	Yes
Huntington (B)	1886	Railroad	Yes
Cornucopia (B)	1886	Mining	No
Haines (B)	1886	Railroad	Yes
Alder (W)	1886	R.S.C.	No
Enterprise (W)	1886	Co. Seat	Yes
Hilgard (U)	1888	Lumber	No
Sumpter (B)	1889	Mining	Yes
Wallowa (W)	1889	R.S.C.	Yes

*County abbreviations: (B) Baker; (U) Union; (W) Wallowa.
†Date of post office establishment is used as date of founding for unplatted towns.
‡Economic base indicates the base at the time of town founding. In the case of some railroad towns, the railroad provided the motivation for platting but the true effective base was as a rural service center (R.S.C.).

Source: Plat Books, Baker, Union and Wallowa counties. McArthur, *Oregon Geographic Names* (1974).

190

TABLE 6
HINTERLAND TOWNS FOUNDED 1890-1915

NAME	PLAT DATE	ECONOMIC BASE‡	STILL A TOWN IN 1980?
Alicel (U)*	1890	Railroad	No
Imbler (U)	1891	Railroad	Yes
McEwen (B)	1891	Railroad	No
Unity (B)	1891 (P.O.)†	R.S.C.	Yes
Middletown (U)	1894	Road	No
Flora (W)	1897	R.S.C.	No
Richland (B)	1897	R.S.C.	Yes
Burkemont (B)	1900	Mining	No
Carson (B)	1900	R.S.C.	No
Whitney (B)	1900	Lumber	No
Bourne (B)	1902	Mining	No
Imnaha (W)	1902 (P.O.)	R.S.C.	Yes
Pleasant Valley (B)	1903	Railroad	No
Rock Creek (B)	1903	R.S.C.	No
Tipton (B)	1904	Lumber	No
Greenhorn (B)	1904	Mining	No
Langrell (B)	1906	R.S.C.	Yes
Copperfield (B)	1907	Railroad	No
Minam City (U)	1907	Railroad	No
Ballard (B)	1907	Ferry	No
Halfway (B)	1907 (P.O.)	R.S.C.	Yes
Durkee (B)	1908	Railroad	Yes
New Bridge (B)	1908	R.S.C.	No
Robinette (B)	1908	Railroad	No
Homestead (B)	1909	Mining	No
Evans (W)	1910	Railroad	No
Troy (W)	1910	Ferry	Yes
Radium (B)	1913	Railroad	No

*County Abbreviations: (B) Baker; (U) Union; (W) Wallowa.
†Date of post office establishment is used as date of founding for unplatted towns.
‡Rural Service Center.

Source: Plat Books, Baker, Union and Wallowa counties. McArthur, *Oregon Geographic Names* (1974).

TABLE 7
BAKER, UNION AND WALLOWA COUNT

TOWN	DATE EST.	1873	1880	1890	1900
Bridgeport (B)†	1862 (P.O.)‡	100			
Clarksville (B)	1862 (P.O.)	200			
Baker (B)	1864	1000	1258	2604	6663
Union (U)	1864	250	416	604	1600
La Grande (U)	1868	550	520	2583	2991
Sparta (B)	1872 (P.O.)	300	213	150	
Summerville (U)	1873	100	350	280	184
Cove (U)	1874	20	250	223	350
Island City (U)	1874		100	145	150
Joseph (W)	1883			249	237
Lostine (W)	1884			50	150
Telocaset (U)	1885 (P.O.)			25	
North Powder (U)	1885			185	150
Elgin (U)	1886			227	603
Huntington (B)	1886			320	821
Cornucopia (B)	1886			150	400
Haines (B)	1886			200	150
Enterprise (W)	1888			242	396
Hilgard (U)	1888			429	400
Sumpter (B)	1889			85	1809
Wallowa (W)	1889			30	243
Alicel (U)	1890			40	
Imbler (U)	1891			50	80
Unity (B)	1891 (P.O.)				
Flora (W)	1897			36	75
Richland (B)	1897				100
Burkemont (B)	1900				
Carson (B)	1900				
Whitney (B)	1900				
Bourne (B)	1902				
Imnaha (W)	1902 (P.O.)			25	25
Rock Creek (B)	1903				
Homestead (B)	1904				
Greenhorn (B)	1904				
Copperfield (B)	1907				
Halfway (B)	1907 (P.O.)				60
Durkee (B)	1908			42	75
New Bridge (B)	1908				45
Robinette (B)	1908				
Evans (W)	1910				
Troy (W)	1910				

*No population data available for Auburn (B, P.O. 1862), Oro Dell (U, 1868), Alder (W 1886), McEwen (B, 1891), Middletown (U, 1894), Pleasant Valley (B, 1903), Tipton (B, 1904), Langrell (B, 1906), Minam City (U, 1907) and Ballard (U, 1907).
†County abbreviations: (B) Baker; (U) Union; (W) Wallowa.
‡Post office establishment is used as the date of founding for unplatted towns.

OWN POPULATIONS*

1910	1920	1930	1940	1950	1960	1970	1980
6742	7729	7858	9342	9471	9986	9354	9471
1483	1319	1107	1398	1307	1490	1531	2062
4843	6913	8050	7747	8635	9014	9645	11354
152		100					
237	116	116	80	73	76	76	132
433	399	307	321	282	311	363	451
166	141	116	177	138	158	202	477
725	770	504	593	666	788	839	999
230	244	176	204	178	240	196	250
75		45					
455	613	553	376	403	399	304	430
1120	1043	728	997	1223	1315	1375	1701
680	666	803	744	733	689	507	539
150	100	10	355				
423	503	431	377	321	331	314	341
1242	1895	1379	1709	1718	1932	1680	2003
200	150	150	50	25	25	35	NA§
643	219	154	420	146	96	120	133
793	894	749	838	1055	989	811	847
200	206	203	182	149	137	139	292
							115
200	218	50	50	50	30	20	NA
334	244	212	254	220	228	133	181
20							
45							
55	97	36	19				
77	250	30	19				
50	50	26	25	25	25	25	NA
30							
25		50					
28	5	11	5				3
250	155	75					
183	350	351	416	312	505	317	380
100	100	100	100	100	100	90	NA
35	40	26	25	25	25	50	NA
20		5					
	100						
20	25	25	25	25	25	25	NA

§NA: Not available.
Source: Population figures for incorporated towns are from U.S. Census; for unincorporated towns, from business directories. Data lacking for Unity prior to 1980. Population figure sequences rounded off to nearest 10 or 25 prior to 1980 are author's estimates.

TABLE 8
TOWN FOUNDING AND GROWTH
ORIGINAL PLATS AND PLATTED ADDITIONS*

Union	*1864*, 1865, 1874, 1876, 1878, 1879, 1882, 1890 (2), 1892, 1928, 1971, 1973	Wallowa	*1889*, 1893, 1899, 1901, 1906, 1907 (2), 1909 (2), 1910 (2), 1911
Oro Dell	*1868*	Alicel	*1890*
Summerville	*1873*, 1874	Imbler	*1891*, 1972
Cove	*1874*, 1884 (2), 1896, 1900, 1906	McEwen	*1891*
		Middletown	*1894*
Island City	*1874*, 1879, 1880, 1891, 1967, 1968, 1969, 1970, 1975	Flora	*1897*, 1923
		Richland	*1897*, 1900, 1901 (2), 1907
Joseph	*1883*, 1888 (2), 1889, 1901 (2), 1902, 1907 (2), 1909, 1913	Burkemont	*1900*
		Carson	*1900*
		Whitney	*1900*, 1901
		Bourne	*1902*
Lostine	*1884*, 1897, 1900, 1950 (2)	Pleasant Valley	*1903*
		Rock Creek	*1903*, 1904
North Powder	*1885*, 1908	Tipton	*1904*
Elgin	*1886*, 1888, 1890 (3), 1891, 1897, 1904, 1956	Greenhorn	*1904*
		Langrell	*1906*
		Copperfield	*1907*
Huntington	*1886*, 1891	Minam City	*1907*
Cornucopia	*1886*	Ballard	*1907*
Haines	*1886*, 1904, 1912 (2)	Durkee	*1908*
Alder	*1886*	New Bridge	*1908*, 1909
Enterprise	*1886*, 1887, 1888 (5), 1900, 1901, 1903, 1905, 1907 (5), 1908, 1909 (2), 1913, 1914, 1915 (2), 1916 (7), 1917 (3), 1918	Robinette	*1908*
		Halfway†	*1908*, 1909, 1911 (3), 1916 (3), 1918
		Homestead	*1909*, 1916
		Evans	*1910*
		Troy	*1910*
		Radium	*1913*
Hilgard	*1888*		
Sumpter	*1889*, 1895, 1897 (3), 1898, 1899 (9), 1902 (2), 1903		

---

*Date in italics indicates original plat. Number in parentheses indicates how many additions were platted in that year if there were more than one.

†Halfway original town unplatted, first platted addition 1908.

Source: Plat Books and Deed Registers, Baker, Union, and Wallowa counties.

TABLE 9
TOTAL BUSINESS ESTABLISHMENTS OF FOUR SELECTED MAIN STREETS*

Commercial Activities	1900	1910
General Store	15	11
Dry goods	1	3
Dry goods and clothing		2
Grocery	5	3
Gentlemen's furnishings	2	2
Clothing		2
Boots and shoes	3	2
Store	4	9
Meat	5	5
Bakery	1	5
Confectionary	4	11
Drugs	7	9
Bank	4	6
Hardware	4	5
Tin shop	3	4
Stoves	1	1
Furniture	4	7
Picture framing		
Paints, oils, wallpaper	1	4
Restaurant	4	5
Saloon	11	2
Saloon and billiards		3
Billiards	1	5
Cigars, tobacco	1	
Jewelry	1	5
Notions	4	1
Stationery	2	3
2nd hand store		1
Agricultural implements		

Lodgings	1900	1910
House	12	7
Hotel	5	6
Boarding	1	
Lodgings on 2nd	2	2

Transportation	1900	1910
Livery	4	3
Livery and feed	1	1
Stage barn	1	
Blacksmith	7	6
Wagon shop		2
Harness	5	6
Garage		

Services	1900	1910
Post Office	4	3
Telephone office	1	5
Hand printing	3	1
Printing		3
Barber	6	6
Cobbler		
Millinery	8	6
Carpenter		3
Chinese laundry	1	
Cleaning and pressing		2
Insurance office		3
Doctor's office		4
Dentist's office	1	
Photographer	3	3
Office	8	9
Offices on 2nd	4	2

Other	1900	1910
Brewery		
Lodge hall on 2nd	3	4
Dance hall		2
Opera House	1	2
Bowling alley	2	
Shooting gallery	1	
Moving pictures		2
Vacant	4	

Elgin, Enterprise, Joseph and Union. 1900 population totals: towns, 2,836; census divisions, 7,888. 1910 totals: towns, 4,570; census divisions, 10,502.

Source: Sanborn Map Company, "Elgin" (1900, 1910), "Enterprise" (1900, 1910), "Joseph" (1901, 1910), "Union" (1900, 1910).

TABLE 10
BUSINESS COMMUNITY SIZE AND STABILITY

	Date of Business Directory								
	1873	1881	1891	1901	1913	1923	1926	1932	Total
STAGE 2 TOWNS:									
SUMMERVILLE									
Total names*	9	28	32	22	11	—	3	2	107
Old names		2	6	8	4	—	2	2	24
New names		26	26	14	7	—	1	0	74
Gone		7	22	24	18	—	9	1	81
RICHLAND									
Total names				22	27	28	15	11	103
Old names					5	7	9	5	26
New names					22	21	6	6	55
Gone					17	20	19	10	66
FLORA									
Total names					16	6	5	2	29
Old names						2	3	2	7
New names						4	2	0	6
Gone						14	3	3	20
STAGE 3 TOWNS:									
WALLOWA									
Total names			6	50	36	42	35	30	199
Old names				0	7	12	16	12	47
New names				50	29	30	19	18	146
Gone				6	43	24	26	23	122
NORTH POWDER									
Total names			21	24	30	34	26	18	153
Old names				4	5	9	14	7	39
New names				20	25	25	12	11	93
Gone				17	19	21	20	19	96
HUNTINGTON									
Total names			45	47	26	24	17	20	179
Old names				9	5	7	6	8	35
New names				83	21	17	11	12	99
Gone				36	42	20	18	9	125

				Date of Business Directory					
	1873	**1881**	**1891**	**1901**	**1913**	**1923**	**1926**	**1932**	**Total**

STAGE 4 TOWNS:

UNION
Total names	8	44	98	81	48	38	37	30	384
Old names		5	13	23	10	12	15	13	91
New names		39	85	58	38	26	22	17	285
Gone		3	31	78	71	36	23	24	266

ENTERPRISE
Total names			65	61	61	119	73	57	436
Old names				6	8	23	35	25	97
New names				55	53	96	38	32	274
Gone				59	53	38	84	48	282

ELGIN
Total names			78	69	36	39	26	24	272
Old names				13	12	7	14	17	63
New names				56	24	32	12	7	131
Gone				65	57	29	25	9	185

SUMPTER
Total names			17	166	59	1	5	2	250
Old names				0	9	0	0	2	11
New names				166	50	1	5	0	222
Gone									

---

*Total names: total number of names in business community listed in directory.

Old names: number of names repeated from preceding directory.

New names: number of names appearing for first time in directory.

Gone: number of names that disappeared between preceding and current directory.

Source: Oregon Business Directory (1873), *Oregon State Directory* (1881), *Oregon . . . Business Directory* (1891, 1901, 1913), *Polk's Oregon . . . Business Directory* (1923), *Bradstreet's Book of Commercial Ratings* (1926, 1932).

TABLE 11
BUSINESS BASE IN NINE SELECTED TOWNS
1870-1930*

TOWNS	TOWN RESIDENTS: BUSINESSMEN						
	1870	1880	1890	1900	1910	1920	1930
Stage 2	11.1	12.5	8.8	6.5	20.2	17.0	25.2
Stage 3	—	—	7.4	10.0	19.7	21.7	30.6
Stage 4	31.3	9.5	4.5	12.3	26.5	21.7	28.6

HINTERLANDS	RURAL RESIDENTS: BUSINESSMEN						
	1870	1880	1890	1900	1910	1920	1930
Stage 2	24.4	36.1	46.5	42.7	32.7	42.2	87.6
Stage 3	—	—	19.0	14.2	26.8	26.2	36.0
Stage 4	18.7	16.4	11.4	12.9	22.7	16.0	30.4

TOTAL	RESIDENTS: BUSINESSMEN						
	1870	1880	1890	1900	1910	1920	1930
Stage 2	35.5	48.6	55.3	49.2	52.9	59.2	112.8
Stage 3	—	—	26.4	24.2	46.5	47.9	66.6
Stage 4	50.0	25.9	15.9	25.2	49.2	37.7	59.0

*Nine towns: Elgin, Enterprise, Flora, Huntington, North Powder, Richland, Summerville, Union, Wallowa.

Source: Population data from *Oregon Business Directory* (1873) and *U.S. Census of Population* (1880-1930). Businessmen numbers from the business directory closest in publishing date to U.S. decennial census.

TABLE 12
TOTAL OF MAIN STREET BUSINESSES
IN EIGHT TOWNS, 1910-11*

Commercial Activities	Number		Number
General store	22	**Transportation**	
Dry goods	2	Livery	9
Dry goods and clothing	2	Livery and feed	2
Grocery	2	Stage barn	
Gentlemen's furnishings	2	Blacksmith	10
Clothing		Wagon shop	5
Boots and shoes	2	Harness	7
Meat	10	Garage	1
Bakery	5		
Confectionery	14	**Services**	
Drugs	13	Post Office	8
Bank	8	Telephone office	5
Hardware	9	Hand printing	2
Tin shop	4	Printing	5
Stoves	2	Newspaper	
Furniture	7	Photographer	3
Picture framing	2	Barber	9
Paints, oils, wallpaper	8	Cobbler	3
Restaurant	8	Millinery	9
Saloon	10	Carpenter	3
Saloon and billiards	6	Cleaning and pressing	5
Billiards	8	Insurance office	5
Cigars, tobacco		Doctor's office	6
Jewelry	4	Dentist's office	
Notions	1	Office	7
Stationery	1	Office on 2nd	1
2nd hand store	1	Plumbing	2
Agricultural implements	4	Undertaker	3
Chinese goods	1		
Store	20	**Other**	
		Sausage factory	3
Lodgings		Brewery	1
		Dance hall	2
Hotel	8	Opera House	2
Boarding	2	Moving pictures	2
Lodgings	3	Lodge hall	8
Lodgings on 2nd	6	Vacant	7

*Elgin, Enterprise, Huntington, North Powder, Richland, Summerville, Union, Wallowa.

Source: Sanborn Map Company, "Elgin" (1910), "Enterprise" (1910), "Huntington" (1911), "North Powder" (1910), "Richland" (1911), "Summerville" (1910), "Union" (1910), "Wallowa" (1910).

TABLE 13
MAIN STREET BUSINESSMEN PERSISTENCE AN

	Number		
	1901	**1913**	**1923**
Commercial Activities			
General store	12	18	17
Dry goods			
Dry goods and clothing			1
Grocery		1	2
Gentlemen's furnishings			
Clothing			
Boots and shoes	1		
Meat	1	1	
Bakery			
Confectionery			
Drugs	3	4	3
Bank	5	5	5
Hardware	1	1	2
Tin shop			
Stoves			
Furniture	1	2	6
Picture framing			
Paints, oils, wallpaper			
Restaurant			
Saloon	1		
Saloon and billiards			
Billiards			
Cigars, tobacco			
Jewelry	1	1	2
Notions			
Stationery			
2nd hand store	1		
Chinese goods		1	1
Agricultural implements			
Transportation			
Livery	4	2	
Livery and feed			
Stage barn			
Blacksmith	2		
Wagon shop	1		
Harness	2	1	
Garage			3

Towns: 1901—Elgin, Enterprise, Huntington, North Powder, Summerville, Union, Wallowa; 1913—The above, plus Richland; 1923—All of the above, plus Flora.
Total Names: 1901—354; 1913—275; 1923—330.
Old Names: 1901—63; 1913—56; 1923—79.

	Number		
	1901	**1913**	**1923**
Lodgings			
Hotel	1	2	3
Boarding			
Services			
Post Office	2	2	2
Telephone office			
Hand printing			
Printing			
Newspaper	1		2
Photographer			
Barber	2		2
Cobbler			
Millinery		1	
Carpenter			
Brick maker	1		
Painter	1		
Plasterer	1		
Cleaning, pressing			
Insurance agent	2		1
Real estate agent		2	5
Doctor	3	4	6
Dentist			2
Lawyer	2	2	6
Public official	4		1
Railroad agent	2		
Electric company			1
Other			
Sausage factory			
Brewery	1		
Dance hall	1		
Opera House			
Moving pictures			
Planing mill	1	1	
Saw mill	1	3	3
Other			5

Source: Oregon ... Business Directory (1891, 1901, 1913), *Polk's Oregon ... Business Directory* (1923).

Notes

1. Wilson Price Hunt, "Journey of Mr. Hunt and His Companions from Saint Louis to the Mouth of the Columbia by a New Route Across the Rockey Mountains," Philip Ashton Rollins, ed., *The Discovery of the Oregon Trail; Robert Stuart's Narratives* (New York, 1936), p. 300.

2. Donald Jackson and Mary Lee Spence, *The Expeditions of John Charles Frémont*, vol. 1 (Urbana, Illinois, 1970), p. 543.

3. Jackson and Spence, *The Expeditions of John Charles Frémont*, p. 545.

4. Jackson and Spence, *The Expeditions of John Charles Frémont*, p. 547.

5. "Romantic Days of Fur Trappers Recounted," *Evening Observer* (La Grande), 15 September 1938.

6. Lewis A. McArthur, *Oregon Geographic Names,* 4th ed., revised and enlarged by Lewis L. McArthur (Portland, 1974), p. 239.

7. Bernal Hug, *History of Union County, Oregon* (La Grande, 1961), p. 27.

8. *An Illustrated History of Union and Wallowa Counties* (Spokane, 1902).

9. Hug, *History of Union County*, p. 63.

10. Dietrich Deumling, "The Roles of the Railroad in the Development of the Grande Ronde Valley" (Master's thesis, Northern Arizona State University, 1972).

11. Eastern Oregon Community Development Council, "Net Volume of Growing Stock and Sawtimber on Commercial Timberland, January 1, 1973," *The Other Side of the Mountains* (La Grande, 1975), p. 13-3.

12. Eastern Oregon Community Development Council, "Labor Force by County," *The Other Side of the Mountains*, p. 15-2.

13. Interview with Cressie Green, Enterprise, 14 March 1976 (Mrs. Green grew up on a homestead on Crow Creek).

14. Evans Smith McComas, *A Journal of Travel* (Portland, 1954).

15. *Oregon Business Directory* (Portland, 1873), p. 336.

16. Oscar Osburn Winther, *The Old Oregon Country* (Stanford, 1950), p. 258.

17. Union County. Deed Register (1864), Book A, p. 32.

18. Union County. Deed Register (1873-1822), Books 1, B-G.

19. Interview with John Evans, January, 1976.

Bibliography

Published Sources

Berry, Brian J. L. *Geography of Market Centers and Retail Distribution*. Englewood Cliffs, N.J., 1967.

Berry, Brian J. L., Barnum, H. G. and Tennant, R. H. "Retail Location and Consumer Behavior." *Papers and Proceedings, Regional Science Association*, vol. 9 (1962): 65-106.

Berry, Brian J. L. and Garrison, William L. "Functional Bases of the Central Place Heirarchy." *Economic Geography* 34 (1958): 145-54.

Blue Mountain American (Sumpter, published weekly). 15 September, 25 November, 2 December 1915; 5 January 1916; 28 July, 16 August 1917.

Bowden, Martyn J. "Downtown Through Time: Delimitation, Expansion, and Internal Growth." *Economic Geography* 17 (April, 1971): 121-23.

Bradstreet's Book of Commercial Ratings. New York, 1915, 1926, 1932.

Brush, John E. and Bracey, Howard E. "Rural Service Centers in Southwestern Wisconsin and Southern England." *Geographical Review* 45 (October, 1955): 559-69.

Burch, Albert. "Development of Metal Mining in Oregon." *Oregon Historical Quarterly* 43 (June, 1942): 105-28.

Burr, Walter. *Small Towns: An Estimate of Their Trade and Culture*. New York, 1929.

Butterfield, Grace and Horner, J. H. "Wallowa Valley Towns and Their Beginnings." *Oregon Historical Quarterly* 41 (1940): 382-85.

Center for Population Research and Census. *Population Estimates of Counties and Incorporated Cities of Oregon*. Portland, 1975.

Chittick, Douglas. *Growth and Decline of South Dakota Trade Centers, 1901-1915*. South Dakota Agricultural Station Bulletin 448. Brookings, 1955.

Colladay, Morrison. "The Passing of the American Village." *Commonweal* 56 (1952): 363-64.

Conzen, Michael P. "The Maturing Urban System in the United States, 1840-1910." *Annals of the Association of American Geographers* 67 (June, 1977): 88-108.

Eagle Valley News (Richland, published weekly). 25 June, 9 July, 23 August 1914.

Eastern Oregon Community Development Council. *The Other Side of the Mountains: A Statistical Handbook of Northeast Oregon*. La Grande, 1975.

Eide, Ingvard Henry. *Oregon Trail*. Chicago, 1972.

Ensminger, Douglas and Longmore, T. Wilson. "Rural Trade Areas and Villages." In *Rural Life in the United States*, edited by Carl C. Taylor et al. New York, 1949.

Fletcher, Henry J. "The Doom of the Small Town." *Forum* 19 (April, 1895): 214-23.

Flora Journal (Flora, published weekly). 4 July 1902.

Forbes, D. "Central Place Theory—An Analytical Framework for Retail Structure." *Land Economics* 58 (February, 1971):15-22.

Franklin, Jerry F. and Dyrness, C. T. *Natural Vegetation of Oregon and Washington*. U.S.D.A. Forest Service General Technical Report PNW-8. Portland, 1973.

Fuguitt, Glenn V. "County Seat Status as a Factor in Small Town Growth and Decline." *Social Forces* 44 (December, 1965): 245-51.

Gaston, Joseph. "The Genesis of the Oregon Railway System." *Oregon Historical Quarterly* 7 (1906): 105-32.

Gilluly, James, Reed, J. C. and Park, C. F. *Some Mining Districts of Eastern Oregon*. U.S. Geological Survey Bulletin 846-A. Washington, D.C., 1933.

Glassie, Henry. *Pattern in the Material Folk Culture of the Eastern United States*. Philadelphia, 1968.

Hill, James M. *The Mining Districts of the Western United States*. U.S. Geological Survey Bulletin 507. Washington, D.C., 1912.

Hug, Bernal D. *History of Union County, Oregon*. La Grande, 1961.

Hunt, Wilson Price. "Journey of Mr. Hunt and His Companions from Saint Louis to the Mouth of the Columbia by a New Route Across the Rockey Mountains." In *The Discovery of the Oregon Trail; Robert Stuart's Narratives*, edited by Philip Ashton Rollins. New York, 1936.

An Illustrated History of Baker, Grant, Malheur, and Harney Counties. Spokane, 1902.

An Illustrated History of Union and Wallowa Counties. Spokane, 1902.

Jackson, Donald and Spence, Mary Lee. *The Expeditions of John Charles Frémont*, vol. 1. Urbana, Illinois, 1970.

Jenson, Oliver, Paterson, Joan and Belsky, Murray, eds. *American Album*. New York, 1968.

Johnson, Lee C. "History of Union County." *Evening Observer* (La Grande). 14 May 1949 (Union County History Edition).

Kenyon, James B. "On the Relationship Between Central Place Function and Size of Place." *Annals of the Association of American Geographers* 57 (December, 1967): 736-50.

Kniffen, Fred and Glassie, Henry. "Building in Wood in the Eastern United States." *Geographical Review* 56 (March, 1966): 40-56.

Landis, Paul H. *Washington Trade Centers 1900-1935*. Washington Agricultural Experiment Station Bulletin 360. Pullman, Washington, 1938.

Lloyd, W.W. and Melhorn, Edna A. "Baker County Historical Society." *Oregon Historical Quarterly* 49 (1948): 306-7.

Lomax, Alfred L. *Pioneer Woolen Mills in Oregon*. Portland, 1941.

McArthur, Lewis A. *Oregon Geographic Names*. 4th edition, revised and enlarged by Lewis L. McArthur. Portland, 1974.

McComas, Evans Smith. *A Journal of Travel*. Portland, 1954.

Martin, R. R. "Village Changes in the Pacific Northwest." *Social Forces* 15 (May, 1937): 536-43.

Meinig, D. W. *The Great Columbia Plain*. Seattle, 1968.

Metsker, Charles F. *Metsker's Atlas of Baker County*. Portland, 1952.

"Mining in Eastern Oregon." *The Mining World*, 27 May 1911.

Nelson, Howard J. "Town Founding and the American Frontier." *Yearbook of the Association of Pacific Coast Geographers* 36 (1974): 7-23.

Oregon Business Directory. Portland, 1973.

Oregon Historical Society, comp. "Oregon Ghost Towns and some Historic Communities" (pamphlet). Portland, 1970.

Oregon Metal Mines Handbook. Oregon Bureau of Mines and Geology. Portland, 1939.

Oregon State Directory. Portland, 1881.

Oregon, Washington and Alaska Gazetteer and Business Directory, 1901-02. Portland, 1901.

Oregon, Washington and Idaho Gazetteer and Business Directory, 1891-92. Portland, 1891.

Oregon and Washington State Gazetteer and Business Directory, 1913-14. Seattle, 1913.

Pease, Robert W. *Modoc County, A Geographic Continuum on the California Volcanic Tableland*. University of California Publications in Geography, vol. 17. Berkeley, 1965.

Pillsbury, Richard. "The Urban Street Pattern as a Culture Indicator: Pennsylvania." *Annals of the Association of American Geographers* 60 (September, 1970): 428-46.

Pine Valley Herald (Halfway, published weekly). 31 January, 26 June, 3 July 1924.

Polk's Oregon and Washington State Gazetteer and Business Directory, 1923-24. Seattle, 1923.

Pomeroy, Earl. "The Urban Frontier of the Far West." In *The Frontier Challenge*, edited by John G. Clark. Lawrence, Kansas, 1971.

Rifkind, Carole. *Main Street: The Face of Urban America*. New York, 1977.

Rollins, Philip Ashton. *The Discovery of the Oregon Trail: Robert Stuart's Narratives*. New York, 1936.

"Romantic Days of Fur Trappers Recounted." *Evening Observer* (La Grande). 13 September 1938.

Stewart, Charles T. "The Size and Spacing of Cities." *Geographical Review* 48 (April, 1958): 201-45.

Swartley, A. M. "Ore Deposits of Northeastern Oregon." *Mineral Resources of Oregon* 1 (December, 1914).

Turner, Frederick Jackson. "The Significance of the Frontier in American History." In *The Frontier in American History*, edited by F. J. Turner. New York, 1920.

U.S., Department of Commerce, Bureau of the Census. *Census of Agriculture*, vol. 1 ("Statistics for Counties"). Washington, D.C., 1900-1980.

U.S., Department of Commerce, Bureau of the Census. *Census of Population*, vol. 1 ("Number of Inhabitants"). Washington, D.C., 1860-1980.

U.S. Weather Bureau. *Climates of the States: Oregon*. Washington, D.C., 1960.

Winther, Oscar Osburn. *The Old Oregon Country*. Stanford, 1950.

Yeates, Maurice H. and Garner, Barry J. *The North American City*. New York, 1971.

Unpublished Sources

Abstract and Title Company. "Index to Abstracts and Titles." La Grande, Oregon.

Baker County. Plat Book, vols. 1-3. Baker County Courthouse, Baker, Oregon.

Baker County. Tax Assessor's Plats: Bridgeport, Clarksville, Cornucopia, Durkee, Halfway, Homestead, Huntington, New Bridge, Richland, Robinette, Sumpter. 1974-76. Baker County Courthouse, Baker, Oregon.

Baker County. Tax Assessor's Rolls: Huntington, Richland, Sumpter. 1974-75. Baker County Courthouse, Baker, Oregon.

Deumling, Dietrich. "The Roles of the Railroad in the Development of the Grande Ronde Valley." Master's thesis, Northern Arizona State University, 1972.

Elmer, William W. "Copy of Report on North Pole-Columbia Lodes, Baker County, Oregon" (30 June 1930). Unpublished manuscript. Oregon Department of Geology and Mineral Industries, Baker, Oregon.

Galloway, J. T. "Book of Sales" (for Elgin lumber mill, 11 July 1885–21 April 1890). In Ethel Chandler personal collection of Elgin memorabilia.

Holtgrieve, Donald Gordon. "Historical Geography of Transportation Routes and Town Populations in Oregon's Willamette Valley." Ph.D. dissertation, University of Oregon, 1973.

Hug, Bernal D. "History of Elgin, Oregon." Typewritten manuscript. Elgin, 1958.

Hug, Bernal D. "The Village Blacksmith." Mimeographed. Union County Historical Society, La Grande, 1961.

Island City Milling and Mercantile Company. "Blotter No. 1" (Record of credit accounts, 11 December 1884–15 May 1885). Oregon Collection, Eastern Oregon State College.

La Grande City Police Department Files. "Parade Permits." August 1974, 1975.

Nipper, Frank, ed. "Huntington's Past, 1860-1954." Mimeographed. Huntington, 1975.

Union County. Deed Register. Union County Courthouse, La Grande.

Union County. Plat Book, vols. 1-4. Union County Courthouse, La Grande.

Union County. Tax Assessor's Plats: Elgin, Island City, North Powder, Summerville, Union. 1974-75. Union County Courthouse, La Grande.

Union County. Tax Assessor's Rolls: Elgin (1974), North Powder (1902-75), Summerville (1902-75), Union (1975). Union County Courthouse, La Grande.

Union Pacific System. "Oregon-Washington Railroad & Navigation Company, First Division, Employes Time Table." n.p., 1927, 1931.

Wallowa County. Deed Register. Original Plats. Wallowa County Courthouse, Enterprise.

Wallowa County. Tax Assessor's Plats: Enterprise, Flora, Joseph, Troy. 1974-75. Wallowa County Courthouse, Enterprise.

Wallowa County. Tax Assessor's Rolls: Enterprise. 1975. Wallowa County Courthouse, Enterprise.

Maps

Baker Development League. "Map of Baker County." Baker City, July, 1906.

Baker Valley Irrigation Company. "The Baker Valley Irrigation Co.'s Map Showing Topography and Drainage Area, Reservoir and Dam Sites, Approximate Alignment of Main Ditches." Baker, 1897.

Nelson, D. W. C. "General Mining Map of Eastern Oregon." Baker, 1923.

"Road Map of Oregon." n.p., ca. 1895. Available at the University of Oregon Map Library, Eugene.

Sanborn Map Company. "Elgin" (1900, 1910, 1930), "Enterprise" (1890, 1900, 1910, 1917, 1923), "Huntington" (1894, 1895, 1911), "Joseph" (1901, 1903, 1910), "La Grande, 'Island City'" (1893, 1903), "North Powder" (1910), "Richland" (1911), "Richland, 'New Bridge'" (1911), "Summerville" (1888, 1890, 1900, 1910), "Sumpter" (1900, 1910), "Union" (1888, 1893, 1894, 1900, 1910), "Wallowa" (1910, 1917, 1930). New York.

U.S.D.A. Forest Service. "Malheur National Forest." Portland, 1972.

———. "Umatilla National Forest." Portland, 1971.

———. "Wallowa-Whitman National Forest." Portland, n.d.

U.S. Geological Survey. Topographic Maps: "Baker City" (1901), "Pine" (1915), "Telocaset" (1906), "Sumpter" (1901).

Index

stone and brick, 92–100, *93,*
95–97
wood-frame, 90–92, *91, 92*
Burkemont, Baker Co., 23, 52
Burnt River Valley, xiii, xiv, 3, 7, 8,
20, 23, 44, 53
Business growth, northeastern
Oregon, 65–67, 74–79
Butte precinct, Wallowa Co., 30, 31

Camp Carson, Union Co., 27
Canneries, 53
Carson, Baker Co., 21, 54, 60
Cattlemen. *See* Ranchers and
ranching
Cayuse Indians, 5
Chapman, John, 85
Chicago, 32
Chinese population, 20, *181*
Clark, William, 5
Clarksville, Baker Co., 20, 43, 44
Clifford district, Baker Co., 22
Columbia River, 12, 14
Copper Butte district, Baker Co., 23
Copperfield, Baker Co., 22, 51, 52,
170
Copper. *See* Mining
Cornucopia, Baker Co., 16, 20, 21,
43–45
main street, *44–45, 156*
modern-day, 169
railroad service, 52, 53
Cove, Union Co., 14f, 25–27, 46, 70
main street development, 82–83
Cracker Creek district, Baker Co.,
20, 21, 32

Divide precinct, Wallowa Co., 30

Dry farming, 5, 35. *See also* Farming
and farmland; Homestead-
ing; Irrigation
Baker Co., 19–21, 23, 51
Wallowa Co., 31
Durkee (Express), Baker Co., 20, 23,
60, 70
main street, 172
stage transfer stop, 51

Eagle Valley, Baker Co., 16, 20–23,
44, 52–54
Economic development, northeastern Oregon, 32–37, 167–70
Elgin, Union Co., 9, 26, 28, 47, *47*
businesses, 76, *124–25, 144–47*
fires, 83
growth, 68, 73, *75*
main street, *75, 151,* 152, 157
business community, 76
development, 83, 95, 105, *106,*
112, 120
modern-day, 169
regional role, 68, *75,* 87, 112
Elgin district. *See* Indian Valley
Elkhorn Mountains, 9, 19–21, 55
Enterprise, Wallowa Co., xiii, 18, 29,
76f
growth, 72, 73
main street
business community, 76
development, 82, 83, 89, 112–
13, *114–19,* 120, 130, *177*
modern-day, *178–79*
regional role, 47, 68, 137f, *177*
Wallowa County Courthouse, 59,
93
Evans, Wallowa Co., 30, 50–51

212

213

219

Colophon

THE TYPEFACE used in this book was named after its originator, John Baskerville of Birmingham, England, a man of diverse talents. Having worked as a stone carver, writing master and japanned goods manufacturer, Baskerville was employed as Cambridge University's printer in 1758 and a year later began to study typefounding. In 1766 he designed this "Transitional" face—with its wide, closely fitting and vertically stressed characters it bridges Old and Modern styles. Baskerville also originated the process of heating paper as it is fed through the press, a step that revolutionized printing production.

Main Street, Northeastern Oregon was manufactured with the assistance of three Portland firms: Irish Setter and Comgroup typeset the text and display. The printing (on 60 lb. Simpson Offset Vellum) was done by Publishers Press of Salt Lake City. For their assistance in producing this volume recognition must also be extended to Northwest artists Julia Suddaby and James Longstreth.

The book was designed by Bruce Taylor Hamilton, assisted by Colleen Campbell and Tracy Ann Robinson.